55 French Recipes for Home

By: Kelly Johnson

Table of Contents

Appetizers:
- French Onion Soup
- Quiche Lorraine
- Gougères (Cheese Puffs)
- Ratatouille Tart
- Escargot in Garlic Butter
- Pissaladière (Caramelized Onion Tart)
- Salade Niçoise
- Coquilles St-Jacques (Scallops Gratin)
- Brandade de Morue (Salt Cod Puree)
- Chicken Liver Pâté

Main Courses:
- **Boeuf Bourguignon (Beef Burgundy)**
- Confit de Canard (Duck Confit)
- Bouillabaisse (Fish Stew)
- Cassoulet
- Beef Wellington
- Sole Meunière
- Poulet Rôti (Roast Chicken)
- Coq au Vin (Chicken in Wine)
- Blanquette de Veau (Veal Stew)
- Quenelles de Brochet (Pike Dumplings)

Side Dishes:
- Gratin Dauphinois (Potato Gratin)
- Ratatouille
- Haricots Verts Amandine (Green Beans with Almonds)
- Provençal Tomato Tart
- Potato Leek Soup (Vichyssoise)
- Lyonnaise Potatoes
- Pommes Anna (Layered Potatoes)
- Grilled Asparagus with Hollandaise Sauce
- Fougasse (Provencal Flatbread)
- Soufflé au Fromage (Cheese Soufflé)

Breads:
- Baguette
- Pain de Campagne (Country Bread)
- Pain Complet (Whole Wheat Bread)
- Pain Poilâne (Sourdough)
- Pain d'Épices (Spice Bread)

Desserts:
- Tarte Tatin
- Crème Brûlée
- Profiteroles with Chocolate Sauce
- Éclairs
- Madeleines
- Charlotte au Chocolat
- Macarons
- Clafoutis
- Pots de Crème
- Baba au Rhum

Pastries:
- Croissants
- Pain au Chocolat
- Palmiers (Elephant Ears)
- Brioche
- Galette des Rois (King Cake)

Cheese and Wine:
- Cheese Fondue
- Raclette
- Fromage Blanc
- Quiche Alsacienne (Alsatian Bacon and Onion Tart)
- Cheese Board with Baguette

Appetizers:

French Onion Soup Recipe

Ingredients:

For the Soup:

- 4 large onions, thinly sliced
- 3 tablespoons unsalted butter
- 2 tablespoons olive oil
- 2 cloves garlic, minced
- 1 teaspoon sugar
- 1/2 cup dry white wine (optional)
- 8 cups beef or vegetable broth
- 2 bay leaves
- Salt and black pepper, to taste

For the Toasted Baguette and Cheese Topping:

- Baguette slices
- Gruyère or Swiss cheese, grated

Instructions:

1. Caramelize the Onions:

- In a large soup pot or Dutch oven, melt the butter and olive oil over medium heat. Add the sliced onions and cook, stirring occasionally, until they are golden brown and caramelized. This process may take about 30-40 minutes.

2. Add Garlic and Sugar:

- Stir in minced garlic and sugar. Cook for an additional 2-3 minutes until the garlic is fragrant.

3. Deglaze with Wine (Optional):

- If using wine, pour it into the pot to deglaze, scraping up any browned bits from the bottom.

4. Add Broth and Seasonings:

- Pour in the beef or vegetable broth. Add bay leaves, salt, and black pepper. Bring the soup to a simmer, then reduce the heat and let it simmer for at least 15-20 minutes to allow the flavors to meld.

5. Toast Baguette Slices:

- While the soup is simmering, preheat the oven and toast the baguette slices until they are golden and crisp.

6. Assemble the Soup Bowls:

- Preheat the broiler. Ladle the hot soup into oven-safe bowls. Place a few toasted baguette slices on top of each bowl.

7. Add Cheese Topping:

- Generously sprinkle grated Gruyère or Swiss cheese over the baguette slices, ensuring they are well covered.

8. Broil Until Cheese is Melted and Golden:

- Place the soup bowls under the broiler until the cheese is melted and bubbly, and it forms a golden brown crust on top.

9. Serve:

- Carefully remove the bowls from the oven, and serve the French Onion Soup hot.

Enjoy this classic French Onion Soup with its rich, savory broth and gooey melted cheese on top of crusty baguette slices!

Quiche Lorraine Recipe

Ingredients:

For the Pie Crust:

- 1 1/4 cups all-purpose flour
- 1/2 cup unsalted butter, cold and diced
- 1/4 teaspoon salt
- 3-4 tablespoons ice water

For the Filling:

- 8 slices bacon, cooked and crumbled
- 1 cup Gruyère or Swiss cheese, shredded
- 1 tablespoon all-purpose flour
- 1 cup heavy cream
- 4 large eggs
- 1/4 teaspoon salt
- 1/4 teaspoon black pepper
- 1/4 teaspoon ground nutmeg (optional)

Instructions:

1. Prepare the Pie Crust:

- In a food processor, pulse the flour, cold diced butter, and salt until the mixture resembles coarse crumbs. Add ice water, one tablespoon at a time, pulsing until the dough comes together. Form the dough into a disk, wrap it in plastic wrap, and refrigerate for at least 30 minutes.

2. Preheat the Oven:

- Preheat your oven to 375°F (190°C).

3. Roll Out the Pie Crust:

- On a floured surface, roll out the chilled pie crust into a circle large enough to fit into a 9-inch pie dish. Transfer the crust to the pie dish, press it into the bottom, and trim any excess. Optionally, prick the bottom with a fork.

4. Prepare the Filling:

- In a bowl, toss the shredded cheese with one tablespoon of flour. Sprinkle the cheese and crumbled bacon over the pie crust.

5. Whisk the Egg Mixture:

- In another bowl, whisk together the heavy cream, eggs, salt, pepper, and nutmeg (if using) until well combined.

6. Pour Egg Mixture:

- Pour the egg mixture over the cheese and bacon in the pie crust.

7. Bake:

- Bake in the preheated oven for about 35-40 minutes or until the quiche is set and the top is golden brown.

8. Cool and Serve:

- Allow the Quiche Lorraine to cool for a few minutes before slicing. Serve warm or at room temperature.

9. Optional: Garnish with Fresh Herbs:

- Garnish the quiche with fresh herbs like chopped chives or parsley before serving.

Enjoy this classic Quiche Lorraine as a delightful brunch or lunch option!

Gougères (Cheese Puffs) Recipe

Ingredients:

- 1 cup water
- 8 tablespoons unsalted butter, cut into pieces
- 1/2 teaspoon salt
- 1 cup all-purpose flour
- 4 large eggs
- 1 1/2 cups grated Gruyère or Emmental cheese
- 1/2 teaspoon Dijon mustard (optional)
- Pinch of cayenne pepper (optional)

Instructions:

1. Preheat the Oven:

- Preheat your oven to 425°F (220°C). Line two baking sheets with parchment paper.

2. Prepare the Dough:

- In a saucepan, combine water, butter, and salt. Bring the mixture to a boil over medium heat. Add the flour all at once and stir vigorously with a wooden spoon until the dough forms a smooth ball and pulls away from the sides of the pan.

3. Cool the Dough:

- Remove the pan from heat and let the dough cool for a couple of minutes.

4. Add Eggs:

- Add the eggs one at a time, beating well after each addition. Make sure each egg is fully incorporated before adding the next one. The dough should be smooth and glossy.

5. Add Cheese and Optional Ingredients:

- Stir in the grated cheese and, if using, the Dijon mustard and cayenne pepper. Mix until the cheese is evenly distributed throughout the dough.

6. Form the Puffs:

- Drop rounded tablespoons of the dough onto the prepared baking sheets, spacing them about 2 inches apart.

7. Bake:

- Bake in the preheated oven for 15-20 minutes or until the gougères are puffed and golden brown.

8. Serve:

- Serve the gougères warm or at room temperature. They are best when freshly baked.

Optional:

- You can add herbs such as thyme or rosemary to the dough for added flavor.
- For a savory twist, you can also incorporate finely chopped cooked bacon into the dough.

Gougères make for a delightful appetizer or snack, and their cheesy, airy goodness is sure to be a hit at any gathering.

Escargot in Garlic Butter Recipe

Ingredients:

- 24 canned or frozen escargot (snails)
- 1/2 cup unsalted butter, softened
- 4 cloves garlic, minced
- 2 tablespoons fresh parsley, finely chopped
- Salt, to taste
- Black pepper, to taste
- Baguette slices, for serving

Instructions:

1. Preheat the Oven:

- Preheat your oven to 400°F (200°C).

2. Prepare the Escargot:

- If using canned escargot, drain and rinse them thoroughly. If using frozen escargot, ensure they are fully thawed.

3. Make the Garlic Butter:

- In a bowl, combine softened butter, minced garlic, chopped parsley, salt, and black pepper. Mix until well blended.

4. Assemble the Escargot:

- Place each escargot in its shell, and then spoon a small amount of the garlic butter mixture over each one.

5. Bake:

- Arrange the escargot shells in an ovenproof dish or escargot pan. Bake in the preheated oven for about 10-12 minutes or until the butter is bubbly and the escargot are heated through.

6. Serve:

- Serve the escargot hot from the oven. Provide baguette slices on the side for dipping into the delicious garlic butter.

7. Optional: Escargot Tongs and Forks:

- If you have escargot tongs and forks, use them to hold the shells in place while you extract the escargot with the fork.

8. Enjoy:

- Enjoy this classic French delicacy as an appetizer or part of a special meal. The garlic butter adds rich flavor to the tender escargot.

Note:

- Escargot can be found in the canned or frozen section of specialty grocery stores. If using canned escargot, you may want to use escargot shells or small baking dishes for an elegant presentation. If using frozen escargot, follow the package instructions for thawing.
- This dish is often served with a side of crusty bread to soak up the flavorful garlic butter.

Pissaladière (Caramelized Onion Tart) Recipe

Ingredients:

For the Dough:

- 2 1/2 cups all-purpose flour
- 1 teaspoon active dry yeast
- 1 teaspoon sugar
- 1 cup warm water
- 2 tablespoons olive oil
- 1/2 teaspoon salt

For the Topping:

- 4 large onions, thinly sliced
- 3 tablespoons olive oil
- 2 cloves garlic, minced
- 1 teaspoon dried thyme
- Salt and black pepper, to taste
- 1/2 cup black olives, pitted and halved
- 8-10 anchovy fillets in oil
- Fresh thyme leaves for garnish (optional)

Instructions:

1. Prepare the Dough:

- In a small bowl, combine warm water, sugar, and yeast. Let it sit for about 5-10 minutes until it becomes frothy. In a large bowl, mix flour and salt. Make a well in the center and pour in the yeast mixture and olive oil. Mix until the dough comes together. Knead the dough on a floured surface for about 5-7 minutes until it is smooth and elastic. Place the dough in a lightly oiled bowl, cover it with a clean kitchen towel, and let it rise in a warm place for 1-2 hours or until doubled in size.

2. Preheat the Oven:

- Preheat your oven to 400°F (200°C).

3. Caramelize the Onions:

- In a large skillet, heat olive oil over medium heat. Add sliced onions and cook, stirring occasionally, until the onions are soft and caramelized. This process may take about 20-25 minutes. Add minced garlic, dried thyme, salt, and black pepper during the last few minutes of cooking.

4. Roll Out the Dough:

   - Roll out the risen dough on a floured surface to fit your tart pan or baking sheet. Transfer the rolled-out dough to the pan.

5. Assemble the Tart:

   - Spread the caramelized onion mixture evenly over the rolled-out dough. Arrange black olive halves and anchovy fillets on top.

6. Bake:

   - Bake in the preheated oven for approximately 20-25 minutes or until the edges are golden brown and the toppings are cooked.

7. Garnish and Serve:

   - Optionally, garnish with fresh thyme leaves. Let the Pissaladière cool slightly before slicing. Serve warm or at room temperature.

Enjoy this traditional Pissaladière as a flavorful appetizer or light meal, highlighting the rich flavors of caramelized onions, olives, and anchovies on a tender crust.

Salade Niçoise Recipe

Ingredients:

For the Salad:

- 1 pound (450g) small red potatoes, boiled and sliced
- 1 pound (450g) green beans, blanched and halved
- 4 large eggs, hard-boiled and halved
- 1 cup cherry tomatoes, halved
- 1/2 cup Niçoise olives
- 1/2 cup red onion, thinly sliced
- 1/4 cup capers, drained
- 2 (6-ounce) cans tuna in olive oil, drained
- Mixed salad greens (e.g., arugula, butter lettuce)

For the Vinaigrette:

- 1/4 cup extra-virgin olive oil
- 2 tablespoons red wine vinegar
- 1 teaspoon Dijon mustard
- 1 clove garlic, minced
- Salt and black pepper, to taste

Optional Garnish:

- Fresh basil or parsley, chopped

Instructions:

1. Prepare the Salad Ingredients:

- Boil the small red potatoes until tender. Blanch the green beans in boiling water for 3-4 minutes, then transfer them to an ice bath to stop the cooking process. Hard-boil the eggs and slice them in half. Halve the cherry tomatoes, thinly slice the red onion, and drain the capers.

2. Assemble the Salad:

- Arrange the mixed salad greens on a large serving platter or individual plates. Arrange the boiled and sliced potatoes, blanched green beans, halved eggs, cherry tomatoes, Niçoise olives, sliced red onion, and capers on top.

3. Add Tuna:

- Break the canned tuna into chunks and scatter it over the salad.

4. Prepare the Vinaigrette:

- In a small bowl, whisk together the olive oil, red wine vinegar, Dijon mustard, minced garlic, salt, and black pepper. Adjust the seasoning to taste.

5. Dress the Salad:

- Drizzle the vinaigrette over the salad or serve it on the side for individual dressing.

6. Garnish:

- Optionally, garnish the salad with chopped fresh basil or parsley for added freshness.

7. Serve:

- Serve the Salade Niçoise immediately, and enjoy this classic French salad as a refreshing and satisfying meal.

Salade Niçoise is a versatile salad, and you can customize it based on your preferences. Feel free to add or omit ingredients to suit your taste.

Coquilles St-Jacques (Scallops Gratin) Recipe

Ingredients:

- 1 pound (450g) fresh scallops, cleaned
- 1/4 cup dry white wine
- 2 tablespoons unsalted butter
- 2 tablespoons all-purpose flour
- 1 cup whole milk
- 1/4 cup heavy cream
- 1/2 cup Gruyère or Swiss cheese, grated
- 1/4 cup Parmesan cheese, grated
- 2 tablespoons fresh parsley, chopped
- Salt and black pepper, to taste
- 1/2 cup fresh breadcrumbs (optional, for topping)
- Lemon wedges, for serving

Instructions:

1. Prepare the Scallops:

- Pat the scallops dry with paper towels. Season them with salt and black pepper.

2. Sear the Scallops:

- In a large skillet, heat a bit of olive oil over medium-high heat. Sear the scallops for about 1-2 minutes per side until they develop a golden crust. Remove them from the skillet and set aside.

3. Make the White Sauce:

- In the same skillet, melt 2 tablespoons of butter. Add flour and whisk continuously for 1-2 minutes to create a roux. Gradually add the white wine, whole milk, and heavy cream, whisking constantly to avoid lumps. Cook the sauce until it thickens.

4. Add Cheese and Parsley:

- Stir in the grated Gruyère or Swiss cheese, Parmesan cheese, and chopped fresh parsley. Continue to whisk until the cheese is melted and the sauce is smooth.

5. Combine with Scallops:

- Gently fold the seared scallops into the sauce, ensuring they are well coated. Adjust the seasoning with salt and black pepper to taste.

6. Assemble and Bake:

- Preheat your oven to a high broil. Divide the scallop mixture among individual scallop shells or oven-safe dishes. If desired, sprinkle fresh breadcrumbs on top for added texture.

7. Broil Until Golden:

- Place the scallop-filled shells or dishes under the broiler for 2-3 minutes or until the top is golden brown and bubbly.

8. Serve:

- Remove from the oven and let it cool for a minute. Serve the Coquilles St-Jacques hot with lemon wedges on the side.

Enjoy this elegant and creamy Coquilles St-Jacques as an indulgent appetizer or a delightful main course, accompanied by crusty bread or a side of your choice.

Brandade de Morue (Salt Cod Puree) Recipe

Ingredients:

- 1 pound (450g) salted codfish (bacalao), soaked and desalted
- 2 large russet potatoes, peeled and diced
- 1 cup extra-virgin olive oil
- 4 cloves garlic, minced
- 1/4 cup fresh lemon juice
- Salt and black pepper, to taste
- Fresh parsley, chopped (for garnish)
- Baguette slices, for serving

Instructions:

1. Soak and Desalt the Codfish:

- Rinse the salted cod under cold water to remove excess salt. Place it in a large bowl of water and let it soak for at least 24 hours, changing the water several times to desalt the fish.

2. Cook the Codfish:

- Once desalted, place the codfish in a pot of cold water. Bring the water to a simmer and cook the codfish for about 10-15 minutes until it flakes easily. Drain and let it cool.

3. Boil Potatoes:

- Boil the diced potatoes in a separate pot until they are fork-tender. Drain and let them cool slightly.

4. Mash Potatoes and Codfish:

- In a large bowl, mash the cooked potatoes and flake the codfish with a fork. Combine them together.

5. Make the Brandade:

- In a skillet, heat olive oil over medium heat. Add minced garlic and sauté until it becomes fragrant, but not browned. Add this garlic-infused olive oil to the mashed potatoes and codfish mixture, stirring well to combine.

6. Add Lemon Juice and Season:

- Stir in fresh lemon juice and season with salt and black pepper to taste. Adjust the seasoning as needed.

7. Blend Until Smooth:

- For a smoother texture, use an immersion blender or food processor to blend the mixture until it reaches a smooth and creamy consistency.

8. Garnish and Serve:

- Transfer the Brandade de Morue to a serving dish. Garnish with chopped fresh parsley. Serve the salt cod puree warm with baguette slices for spreading.

Enjoy this traditional French dish, Brandade de Morue, as a flavorful spread on crusty bread or as a dip for an appetizer. It's a comforting and rich dish that showcases the unique taste of salted cod.

Chicken Liver Pâté Recipe

Ingredients:

- 1 pound (450g) chicken livers, trimmed and cleaned
- 1/2 cup (1 stick) unsalted butter
- 1 cup finely chopped onions
- 2 cloves garlic, minced
- 1/4 cup brandy or cognac
- 1 teaspoon salt
- 1/2 teaspoon black pepper
- 1/2 teaspoon dried thyme
- 1/2 cup heavy cream
- 2 tablespoons chopped fresh parsley (for garnish)
- Clarified butter (for sealing)

Instructions:

1. Preparing Chicken Livers:

- Trim any connective tissues or greenish parts from the chicken livers. Rinse them under cold water and pat them dry with paper towels.

2. Sautéing Onions and Garlic:

- In a large skillet, melt 1/4 cup of butter over medium heat. Add chopped onions and minced garlic. Sauté until the onions are translucent and soft.

3. Cooking Chicken Livers:

- Add the cleaned chicken livers to the skillet. Cook over medium heat until the livers are browned on the outside but still slightly pink on the inside. This should take about 5-7 minutes.

4. Adding Brandy or Cognac:

- Pour in the brandy or cognac, and let it simmer for 1-2 minutes to allow the alcohol to evaporate.

5. Seasoning:

- Season the mixture with salt, black pepper, and dried thyme. Stir well to combine.

6. Deglazing:

- Deglaze the skillet with heavy cream, scraping any browned bits from the bottom. Simmer for an additional 2-3 minutes.

7. Blending:

- Transfer the mixture to a blender or food processor. Blend until smooth and creamy.

8. Adding Butter:

- While the blender or food processor is running, add the remaining 1/4 cup of butter in small pieces. Blend until the butter is fully incorporated, and the pâté becomes silky.

9. Adjusting Seasoning:

- Taste the pâté and adjust the seasoning if necessary.

10. Straining (Optional):

    - For an extra-smooth texture, you can strain the pâté through a fine-mesh sieve to remove any remaining solids.

11. Portioning:

    - Transfer the pâté into ramekins or small serving dishes.

12. Garnishing:

    - Sprinkle chopped fresh parsley on top for garnish.

13. Sealing with Clarified Butter:

    - Melt clarified butter and pour a thin layer over the top of the pâté. This layer acts as a seal to help preserve the pâté.

14. Chilling:

    - Refrigerate the pâté for at least 4 hours, allowing it to set and develop its flavors.

15. Serving:

    - Serve the chicken liver pâté with toasted bread, crackers, or baguette slices.

16. Enjoy:

- Enjoy this rich and flavorful chicken liver pâté as an appetizer or part of a charcuterie board.

Note:

- Chicken liver pâté can be stored in the refrigerator for up to a week. To extend its shelf life, make sure to keep the surface sealed with clarified butter.

Main Courses:

Boeuf Bourguignon (Beef Burgundy) Recipe

Ingredients:

- 2 pounds (about 1 kg) beef stew meat, cut into chunks
- 4 slices bacon, chopped
- 2 tablespoons olive oil
- 1 large onion, finely chopped
- 2 carrots, peeled and sliced
- 3 cloves garlic, minced
- 2 tablespoons all-purpose flour
- 2 cups red wine (preferably Burgundy)
- 2 cups beef broth
- 2 tablespoons tomato paste
- 1 bouquet garni (a bundle of fresh herbs like thyme, bay leaves, and parsley, tied together)
- Salt and black pepper, to taste
- 1 pound (about 450g) mushrooms, quartered
- 1 cup pearl onions, peeled
- Fresh parsley, chopped (for garnish)
- Mashed potatoes or crusty bread (for serving)

Instructions:

1. Marinate the Beef:

- In a large bowl, marinate the beef chunks with salt, black pepper, and a splash of red wine. Let it marinate for at least 30 minutes or up to overnight in the refrigerator.

2. Sear the Beef:

- In a large Dutch oven or heavy-bottomed pot, heat olive oil over medium-high heat. Remove excess marinade from the beef and sear the meat on all sides until browned. Do this in batches to avoid overcrowding. Remove the seared meat and set it aside.

3. Cook Bacon and Vegetables:

   - In the same pot, add chopped bacon and cook until it renders fat. Add chopped onions, sliced carrots, and minced garlic. Sauté until the vegetables are softened.

4. Add Flour and Deglaze:

   - Sprinkle flour over the vegetables and bacon, stirring to coat evenly. Cook for 1-2 minutes. Pour in a bit of red wine to deglaze the pot, scraping up any browned bits from the bottom.

5. Combine Ingredients:

   - Return the seared beef to the pot. Add the remaining red wine, beef broth, tomato paste, and the bouquet garni. Bring the mixture to a simmer.

6. Simmer and Cook:

   - Reduce the heat to low, cover the pot, and let it simmer for 2 to 2.5 hours or until the beef is tender. Stir occasionally.

7. Sauté Mushrooms and Pearl Onions:

   - In a separate skillet, sauté quartered mushrooms and peeled pearl onions until golden brown. Add them to the pot during the last 30 minutes of cooking.

8. Adjust Seasoning:

   - Taste the Boeuf Bourguignon and adjust the seasoning with salt and black pepper if needed.

9. Garnish and Serve:

   - Remove the bouquet garni. Serve the Boeuf Bourguignon hot, garnished with chopped fresh parsley. It pairs wonderfully with mashed potatoes or crusty bread.

Enjoy this classic French dish, Boeuf Bourguignon, which is rich, hearty, and full of flavor. It's perfect for a cozy family dinner or a special occasion.

Confit de Canard (Duck Confit) Recipe

Ingredients:

- 4 duck leg quarters
- 4 cups duck fat (or a combination of duck fat and vegetable oil)
- 4 cloves garlic, smashed
- 4 sprigs fresh thyme
- 2 bay leaves
- Salt and black pepper, to taste
- 1 tablespoon duck fat (for crisping)
- Fresh parsley, chopped (for garnish, optional)
- Mashed potatoes or crusty bread (for serving)

Instructions:

1. Season the Duck:

- Rinse the duck leg quarters and pat them dry with paper towels. Season generously with salt and black pepper.

2. Marinate:

- Place the duck leg quarters in a dish and add smashed garlic, thyme sprigs, and bay leaves. Cover the dish and let it marinate in the refrigerator for at least 12 hours or overnight.

3. Preheat Oven:

- Preheat your oven to 300°F (150°C).

4. Prepare Confit Mixture:

- In an ovenproof dish or Dutch oven, arrange the marinated duck leg quarters. Melt the duck fat (or duck fat and vegetable oil mixture) until it is completely liquid. Pour the melted fat over the duck legs, ensuring they are fully submerged.

5. Slow Cook:

- Cover the dish with a lid or aluminum foil. Place it in the preheated oven and cook slowly for about 2.5 to 3 hours until the duck is tender and can easily be pulled away from the bone.

6. Crisp the Skin:

- Once the duck is cooked, carefully remove it from the fat. Place the duck leg quarters on a baking sheet. Preheat the oven broiler. Brush the skin of the duck with a bit of reserved duck fat and broil for a few minutes until the skin is crispy. Watch it closely to avoid burning.

7. Serve:

- Serve the Confit de Canard hot, garnished with chopped fresh parsley if desired. It pairs well with mashed potatoes or crusty bread.

8. Optional: Save the Duck Fat:

- Strain and save the duck fat for future use. It can be stored in the refrigerator and used for cooking potatoes or other dishes.

Enjoy this luxurious and flavorful Confit de Canard, a classic French dish known for its tender and succulent duck meat. It's a perfect choice for a special dinner or celebration.

Bouillabaisse (Fish Stew) Recipe

Ingredients:

- 2 pounds (about 900g) mixed fish fillets (such as cod, haddock, snapper), cut into chunks
- 1 pound (about 450g) mixed shellfish (mussels, clams, shrimp), cleaned and debearded
- 1/2 cup olive oil
- 1 large onion, finely chopped
- 2 leeks, cleaned and sliced
- 3 cloves garlic, minced
- 1 fennel bulb, sliced
- 1 large potato, peeled and diced
- 1 cup dry white wine
- 1 (28-ounce) can crushed tomatoes
- 4 cups fish or seafood broth
- 1 teaspoon saffron threads
- 1 bay leaf
- 1 teaspoon dried thyme
- Salt and black pepper, to taste
- Rouille sauce (see recipe below)
- Crusty bread, for serving

Rouille Sauce:

- 1/2 cup mayonnaise
- 2 cloves garlic, minced
- 1 teaspoon Dijon mustard
- 1 teaspoon paprika
- Salt and cayenne pepper, to taste

Instructions:

1. Prepare the Rouille Sauce:

- In a bowl, whisk together mayonnaise, minced garlic, Dijon mustard, paprika, salt, and cayenne pepper. Cover and refrigerate until ready to serve.

2. Prepare the Bouillabaisse:

- In a large pot, heat olive oil over medium heat. Add chopped onion, sliced leeks, minced garlic, and sliced fennel. Sauté until the vegetables are softened.

3. Add Potatoes and Wine:

    - Add diced potatoes to the pot and continue to cook for a few minutes. Pour in the white wine and let it simmer until the alcohol evaporates.

4. Add Tomatoes and Broth:

    - Stir in the crushed tomatoes, fish or seafood broth, saffron threads, bay leaf, and dried thyme. Season with salt and black pepper. Bring the mixture to a simmer.

5. Simmer and Cook:

    - Reduce the heat to low and let the broth simmer for about 15-20 minutes to allow the flavors to meld.

6. Add Fish and Shellfish:

    - Add the fish fillets and shellfish to the pot. Cook until the fish is just opaque and the shellfish have opened. Discard any shellfish that do not open.

7. Adjust Seasoning:

    - Taste the Bouillabaisse and adjust the seasoning with salt and black pepper if needed.

8. Serve:

    - Ladle the Bouillabaisse into bowls. Serve with a dollop of rouille sauce on top and crusty bread on the side.

Enjoy this classic French fish stew, Bouillabaisse, rich with flavors of the sea. The rouille sauce adds a delightful kick, and dipping crusty bread into the broth is a must for the full experience.

Cassoulet Recipe

Ingredients:

- 1 pound (about 450g) dried white beans (such as cannellini or Great Northern), soaked overnight
- 1 pound (about 450g) pork shoulder, cut into chunks
- 4 duck confit legs, or duck legs seasoned with salt and slow-cooked until tender
- 1 pound (about 450g) pork sausages (such as Toulouse sausage), cut into bite-sized pieces
- 1/2 pound (about 225g) pancetta or bacon, diced
- 1 onion, finely chopped
- 4 cloves garlic, minced
- 1 can (14 ounces) crushed tomatoes
- 2 cups chicken or duck broth
- 1 bouquet garni (a bundle of fresh herbs like thyme, bay leaves, and parsley, tied together)
- Salt and black pepper, to taste
- 2 cups fresh breadcrumbs
- 1/2 cup parsley, chopped
- Olive oil, for drizzling

Instructions:

1. Prepare the Beans:

- Drain and rinse the soaked white beans. Place them in a large pot, cover with water, and bring to a boil. Reduce heat, cover, and simmer for about 30-40 minutes or until the beans are just tender. Drain and set aside.

2. Brown the Meats:

- In a large, oven-safe pot, brown the pork shoulder, duck confit legs, pork sausages, and pancetta over medium-high heat. Remove the meats and set them aside.

3. Sauté Onions and Garlic:

- In the same pot, sauté the chopped onion until softened. Add minced garlic and cook for an additional minute.

4. Combine Meats and Tomatoes:

- Return the browned meats to the pot. Add crushed tomatoes, chicken or duck broth, and the bouquet garni. Season with salt and black pepper. Bring the mixture to a simmer.

5. Slow Cook in the Oven:

- Preheat your oven to 325°F (163°C). Cover the pot and transfer it to the preheated oven. Let it cook slowly for about 2 to 2.5 hours or until the meats are tender and the flavors meld.

6. Prepare Breadcrumbs:

- In a separate bowl, mix fresh breadcrumbs with chopped parsley. Set aside.

7. Finish and Serve:

- Once the cassoulet is done cooking, remove the bouquet garni. Sprinkle the breadcrumb mixture over the top of the cassoulet. Drizzle with olive oil.

8. Broil Until Golden:

- Place the cassoulet under the broiler for a few minutes until the breadcrumbs are golden brown.

9. Serve:

- Ladle the cassoulet into bowls and serve hot. Enjoy this hearty French dish with a side of crusty bread.

Cassoulet is a comforting, slow-cooked casserole with a rich combination of meats and beans. It's a classic French dish that's perfect for a cozy family meal or a gathering with friends.

Beef Wellington Recipe

Ingredients:

- 2 to 2.5 pounds (about 1 to 1.25 kg) beef tenderloin
- Salt and black pepper, to taste
- 2 tablespoons olive oil
- 1/2 cup Dijon mustard
- 8-10 slices prosciutto or Parma ham
- 1 pound (about 450g) cremini or button mushrooms, finely chopped
- 4 tablespoons unsalted butter
- 2 cloves garlic, minced
- 1/4 cup dry white wine
- 2 tablespoons fresh thyme, chopped
- Puff pastry sheets (enough to wrap the beef)
- 1 large egg, beaten (for egg wash)
- Salt flakes (for garnish, optional)

Instructions:

1. Prepare the Beef:

- Season the beef tenderloin with salt and black pepper. Heat olive oil in a pan over high heat. Sear the beef on all sides until browned. Let it cool, then brush the entire surface with Dijon mustard.

2. Wrap with Prosciutto:

- Lay out the prosciutto slices slightly overlapping on a sheet of plastic wrap. Place the beef on top and roll it tightly, using the plastic wrap to assist. Chill in the refrigerator while preparing the mushroom duxelles.

3. Make the Mushroom Duxelles:

- In the same pan, melt butter over medium heat. Add minced garlic and cook briefly until fragrant. Add finely chopped mushrooms and cook until they release their moisture. Add white wine and cook until the mixture is dry. Stir in chopped thyme and let it cool.

4. Assemble the Wellington:

- Roll out the puff pastry on a floured surface. Unwrap the prosciutto-wrapped beef and place it in the center. Spread the mushroom duxelles over the prosciutto. Roll the pastry to encase the beef, sealing the edges.

5. Brush with Egg Wash:

- Brush the entire pastry with beaten egg for a golden finish. You can create decorative patterns with the back of a knife if desired.

6. Chill and Preheat Oven:

- Chill the wrapped beef in the refrigerator for at least 30 minutes. Preheat your oven to 400°F (200°C).

7. Bake:

- Place the Beef Wellington on a baking sheet lined with parchment paper. Bake in the preheated oven for about 25-30 minutes or until the pastry is golden brown.

8. Rest and Serve:

- Let the Beef Wellington rest for a few minutes before slicing. Optionally, sprinkle with salt flakes for extra flavor. Serve slices with your favorite accompaniments.

Beef Wellington is a classic dish featuring beef tenderloin encased in puff pastry with a layer of prosciutto and a flavorful mushroom duxelles. This elegant recipe is perfect for special occasions and celebrations.

Sole Meunière Recipe

Ingredients:

- 4 sole fillets (about 6 ounces/170g each), skinless and boneless
- Salt and black pepper, to taste
- All-purpose flour, for dredging
- 4 tablespoons unsalted butter
- 2 tablespoons vegetable oil
- 1 tablespoon fresh lemon juice
- 2 tablespoons fresh parsley, chopped
- Lemon wedges, for serving

Instructions:

1. Prepare the Sole:

- Pat the sole fillets dry with paper towels. Season both sides with salt and black pepper.

2. Dredge in Flour:

- Dredge the sole fillets in flour, shaking off any excess. This creates a light coating that will help achieve a golden brown crust when cooked.

3. Cook the Sole:

- In a large skillet, heat 2 tablespoons of butter and vegetable oil over medium-high heat. When the butter is foamy, add the sole fillets to the pan. Cook for about 2-3 minutes per side or until they are golden brown and cooked through. Be careful not to overcook, as sole fillets are delicate and cook quickly.

4. Transfer and Keep Warm:

- Transfer the cooked sole fillets to a serving platter. Keep them warm.

5. Make the Meunière Sauce:

- In the same skillet, add the remaining 2 tablespoons of butter. Allow it to melt and cook until it turns a light brown color (beurre noisette). Be attentive, as browned butter can quickly turn to burnt butter. Remove the skillet from heat and add fresh lemon juice to the browned butter, swirling to combine.

6. Pour Sauce Over Sole:

- Pour the meunière sauce over the cooked sole fillets, ensuring they are evenly coated.

7. Garnish and Serve:

- Sprinkle the sole with chopped fresh parsley. Serve immediately, garnished with lemon wedges on the side.

8. Serve with Accompaniments:

- Sole Meunière is traditionally served with simple sides like steamed vegetables, boiled new potatoes, or a light salad.

Enjoy this classic French dish, Sole Meunière, known for its delicate flavors and simple preparation that allows the freshness of the sole to shine.

Poulet Rôti (Roast Chicken) Recipe

Ingredients:

- 1 whole chicken (about 4-5 pounds)
- Salt and black pepper, to taste
- 1 lemon, cut in half
- 4-5 sprigs of fresh thyme
- 4 tablespoons unsalted butter, softened
- 2 cloves garlic, minced
- 1 onion, quartered
- 2 carrots, peeled and cut into chunks
- 2 stalks celery, cut into chunks
- Olive oil, for drizzling

Instructions:

1. Preheat the Oven:

    - Preheat your oven to 425°F (220°C).

2. Prepare the Chicken:

    - Pat the chicken dry with paper towels. Season the cavity with salt and black pepper. Place the lemon halves and fresh thyme inside the cavity.

3. Truss the Chicken:

    - Truss the chicken by tying the legs together with kitchen twine. Tucking the wings under the body helps prevent them from burning.

4. Season the Skin:

    - Season the outside of the chicken generously with salt and black pepper. Rub the softened butter over the skin, ensuring it's evenly coated. Sprinkle minced garlic over the butter.

5. Prepare the Vegetables:

- Place the quartered onion, carrot chunks, and celery chunks in the bottom of a roasting pan. Drizzle with olive oil and season with salt and pepper.

6. Roast the Chicken:

- Place the trussed chicken on a rack in the roasting pan, breast side up. Roast in the preheated oven for about 1 hour and 15 minutes or until the internal temperature reaches 165°F (74°C) and the skin is golden brown and crispy.

7. Baste and Rest:

- Baste the chicken with the pan juices every 20-30 minutes. If the skin is getting too dark, cover it loosely with aluminum foil. Once the chicken is done, let it rest for about 15-20 minutes before carving.

8. Carve and Serve:

- Carve the chicken into serving portions. Serve with the roasted vegetables and pan juices.

9. Optional Gravy:

- If desired, you can use the pan drippings to make a simple gravy. Deglaze the pan with a bit of chicken broth or white wine, and thicken with a mixture of flour and water.

Enjoy this classic Poulet Rôti, a French roast chicken dish that is simple, flavorful, and perfect for a comforting family meal or a special occasion.

Coq au Vin (Chicken in Wine) Recipe

Ingredients:

- 1 whole chicken (about 4-5 pounds), cut into serving pieces
- Salt and black pepper, to taste
- 1/2 cup all-purpose flour, for dredging
- 4 tablespoons unsalted butter
- 4 tablespoons olive oil
- 4 slices bacon, chopped
- 12-15 pearl onions, peeled
- 2 carrots, peeled and sliced
- 4 cloves garlic, minced
- 1 bottle (750 ml) red wine (such as Burgundy)
- 2 cups chicken broth
- 2 tablespoons tomato paste
- 1 bouquet garni (a bundle of fresh herbs like thyme, bay leaves, and parsley, tied together)
- 1 pound (about 450g) mushrooms, quartered
- Fresh parsley, chopped (for garnish)

Instructions:

1. Prepare the Chicken:

- Season the chicken pieces with salt and black pepper. Dredge them in flour, shaking off any excess.

2. Brown the Chicken:

- In a large, heavy-bottomed pot or Dutch oven, heat 2 tablespoons of butter and 2 tablespoons of olive oil over medium-high heat. Brown the chicken pieces on all sides. Work in batches if necessary. Remove the browned chicken and set it aside.

3. Sauté Bacon and Vegetables:

- In the same pot, add the chopped bacon and cook until it starts to brown. Add the pearl onions, sliced carrots, and minced garlic. Sauté until the vegetables are softened.

4. Deglaze with Wine:

- Pour in the red wine to deglaze the pot, scraping up any browned bits from the bottom. Allow it to simmer for a few minutes.

5. Add Chicken Broth and Tomato Paste:

- Stir in the chicken broth and tomato paste, ensuring they are well combined.

6. Return Chicken and Add Bouquet Garni:

- Return the browned chicken to the pot. Add the bouquet garni. Bring the mixture to a simmer.

7. Simmer and Cook:

- Reduce the heat to low, cover the pot, and let it simmer for about 1.5 to 2 hours or until the chicken is tender and cooked through.

8. Sauté Mushrooms:

- In a separate skillet, sauté the quartered mushrooms in the remaining 2 tablespoons of butter and 2 tablespoons of olive oil until golden brown. Add the sautéed mushrooms to the pot during the last 30 minutes of cooking.

9. Adjust Seasoning:

- Taste the Coq au Vin and adjust the seasoning with salt and black pepper if needed.

10. Serve:

- Discard the bouquet garni. Serve the Coq au Vin hot, garnished with chopped fresh parsley. It pairs well with mashed potatoes, rice, or crusty bread.

Enjoy this classic French dish, Coq au Vin, which features tender chicken simmered in a rich and flavorful red wine sauce. It's a comforting and elegant dish that's perfect for special occasions.

Blanquette de Veau (Veal Stew) Recipe

Ingredients:

- 2 pounds (about 900g) veal shoulder, cut into chunks
- Salt and black pepper, to taste
- 1/2 cup all-purpose flour, for dredging
- 4 tablespoons unsalted butter
- 1 onion, finely chopped
- 2 carrots, peeled and sliced
- 2 cloves garlic, minced
- 1 bouquet garni (a bundle of fresh herbs like thyme, bay leaves, and parsley, tied together)
- 2 cups chicken broth
- 1 cup dry white wine
- 1 cup mushrooms, quartered
- 1 cup pearl onions, peeled
- 1 cup heavy cream
- 2 tablespoons lemon juice
- Fresh parsley, chopped (for garnish)
- Cooked rice or boiled potatoes (for serving)

Instructions:

1. Prepare the Veal:

- Season the veal chunks with salt and black pepper. Dredge them in flour, shaking off any excess.

2. Brown the Veal:

- In a large, heavy-bottomed pot or Dutch oven, heat 2 tablespoons of butter over medium-high heat. Brown the veal chunks on all sides. Work in batches if necessary. Remove the browned veal and set it aside.

3. Sauté Onion, Carrots, and Garlic:

- In the same pot, add the chopped onion, sliced carrots, and minced garlic. Sauté until the vegetables are softened.

4. Deglaze with Wine:

- Pour in the dry white wine to deglaze the pot, scraping up any browned bits from the bottom. Allow it to simmer for a few minutes.

5. Add Chicken Broth and Bouquet Garni:

- Return the browned veal to the pot. Stir in the chicken broth and add the bouquet garni. Bring the mixture to a simmer.

6. Simmer and Cook:

- Reduce the heat to low, cover the pot, and let it simmer for about 1.5 to 2 hours or until the veal is tender and cooked through.

7. Sauté Mushrooms and Pearl Onions:

- In a separate skillet, sauté the quartered mushrooms and peeled pearl onions in the remaining 2 tablespoons of butter until golden brown. Add them to the pot during the last 30 minutes of cooking.

8. Finish with Cream and Lemon Juice:

- Stir in the heavy cream and lemon juice. Let the blanquette simmer for an additional 10-15 minutes, allowing the flavors to meld.

9. Adjust Seasoning:

- Taste the blanquette de veau and adjust the seasoning with salt and black pepper if needed.

10. Serve:

- Discard the bouquet garni. Serve the blanquette de veau hot, garnished with chopped fresh parsley. It pairs well with cooked rice or boiled potatoes.

Enjoy this classic French dish, Blanquette de Veau, a creamy and tender veal stew that's perfect for a comforting and elegant meal.

Quenelles de Brochet (Pike Dumplings) Recipe

Ingredients:

For the Quenelles:

- 1 pound (about 450g) pike fillets, skinless and boneless
- 1/2 cup fresh breadcrumbs
- 1/2 cup milk
- 2 tablespoons unsalted butter
- 2 egg yolks
- Salt and white pepper, to taste
- Pinch of nutmeg

For the Sauce Nantua:

- 2 tablespoons unsalted butter
- 2 tablespoons all-purpose flour
- 1 cup fish or seafood broth
- 1/2 cup heavy cream
- 1/4 cup white wine
- 1/4 cup crawfish or shrimp tails, cooked
- Salt and white pepper, to taste
- Lemon juice, to taste
- Chopped fresh parsley, for garnish

Instructions:

1. Prepare the Pike Dumplings (Quenelles):

- In a food processor, blend the pike fillets until they form a smooth paste.
- In a saucepan, heat the milk and butter until the butter melts. Add the breadcrumbs and stir to combine. Let it cool slightly.
- Combine the pike paste with the breadcrumb mixture. Add egg yolks, salt, white pepper, and a pinch of nutmeg. Mix until well combined.
- Shape the mixture into oval dumplings using two spoons or your hands dipped in water.
- Poach the quenelles in simmering water for about 10-15 minutes until they are firm and cooked through. Remove them with a slotted spoon and set aside.

2. Prepare the Sauce Nantua:

- In a saucepan, melt butter over medium heat. Add flour and stir to form a roux. Cook for a few minutes until it becomes golden brown.
- Gradually whisk in fish or seafood broth, heavy cream, and white wine. Cook until the sauce thickens.
- Add cooked crawfish or shrimp tails to the sauce. Season with salt, white pepper, and lemon juice to taste.

3. Serve:

- Place the quenelles on a serving dish and pour the Sauce Nantua over them.
- Garnish with chopped fresh parsley.
- Serve the Quenelles de Brochet hot, and they can be accompanied by rice or a side of your choice.

Enjoy this refined French dish, Quenelles de Brochet, showcasing delicate pike dumplings in a creamy and flavorful Sauce Nantua.

Side Dishes:

Gratin Dauphinois (Potato Gratin) Recipe

Ingredients:

- 2 pounds (about 900g) russet potatoes, peeled and thinly sliced
- 2 cups (480ml) whole milk
- 1 cup (240ml) heavy cream
- 2 cloves garlic, peeled and crushed
- 2 cups (about 200g) Gruyère or Emmental cheese, grated
- Salt and white pepper, to taste
- Pinch of nutmeg
- Butter, for greasing the baking dish

Instructions:

1. Preheat the Oven:

- Preheat your oven to 375°F (190°C).

2. Prepare the Potatoes:

- Peel the potatoes and thinly slice them into rounds using a mandoline or a sharp knife.

3. Prepare the Gratin Mixture:

- In a saucepan, combine the whole milk, heavy cream, and crushed garlic. Heat the mixture over medium heat until it is warm but not boiling. Allow the garlic to infuse its flavor into the liquid. Remove the garlic cloves.

4. Assemble the Gratin:

- Butter a baking dish generously. Layer the sliced potatoes evenly in the baking dish.
- Pour the warm milk and cream mixture over the potatoes, ensuring that the liquid covers the potatoes.
- Season with salt, white pepper, and a pinch of nutmeg.

5. Add Cheese:

   - Sprinkle the grated Gruyère or Emmental cheese evenly over the top of the potatoes.

6. Bake:

   - Place the baking dish in the preheated oven and bake for approximately 45-60 minutes or until the potatoes are tender and the top is golden brown.
   - If the top is browning too quickly, you can cover it with foil and continue baking.

7. Serve:

   - Once the Gratin Dauphinois is cooked, remove it from the oven and let it rest for a few minutes before serving.
   - Serve the Gratin Dauphinois as a delicious side dish with roasted meats, poultry, or as part of a festive meal.

Enjoy the creamy and comforting goodness of Gratin Dauphinois, a classic French potato gratin that's perfect for special occasions or as a side dish for a cozy dinner.

Ratatouille Recipe

Ingredients:

- 1 large eggplant, diced
- 2 zucchini, diced
- 1 yellow bell pepper, diced
- 1 red bell pepper, diced
- 1 large onion, finely chopped
- 3 tomatoes, diced
- 4 cloves garlic, minced
- 2 tablespoons tomato paste
- 1/4 cup olive oil
- 1 teaspoon dried thyme
- 1 teaspoon dried oregano
- 1 teaspoon dried rosemary
- Salt and black pepper, to taste
- Fresh basil leaves, for garnish

Instructions:

1. Prepare the Vegetables:

   - Dice the eggplant, zucchini, yellow and red bell peppers, and tomatoes into uniform pieces.

2. Sauté the Onion and Garlic:

   - In a large pan or Dutch oven, heat olive oil over medium heat. Add finely chopped onions and minced garlic. Sauté until the onions are translucent.

3. Add Eggplant and Zucchini:

   - Add diced eggplant and zucchini to the pan. Cook for about 5-7 minutes until they start to soften.

4. Incorporate Bell Peppers and Tomatoes:

   - Stir in the diced red and yellow bell peppers, as well as the diced tomatoes. Cook for an additional 5 minutes.

5. Season and Add Tomato Paste:

   - Season the vegetables with dried thyme, oregano, rosemary, salt, and black pepper. Add tomato paste and mix well.

6. Simmer:

   - Reduce the heat to low, cover the pan, and let the ratatouille simmer for about 20-25 minutes. Stir occasionally to prevent sticking.

7. Check Consistency:

   - Check the consistency of the ratatouille. It should be tender with a rich, flavorful sauce.

8. Garnish:

   - Adjust seasoning if needed. Garnish with fresh basil leaves just before serving.

9. Serve:

   - Serve the ratatouille hot as a side dish, or it can be enjoyed on its own. It pairs well with crusty bread, rice, or pasta.

Ratatouille is a delightful French vegetable stew that celebrates the flavors of summer vegetables. This colorful and aromatic dish is not only a treat for the taste buds but also a feast for the eyes. Enjoy the vibrant and wholesome goodness of homemade ratatouille!

Haricots Verts Amandine (Green Beans with Almonds) Recipe

Ingredients:

- 1 pound (about 450g) haricots verts (French green beans), ends trimmed
- 2 tablespoons unsalted butter
- 1/3 cup sliced almonds
- 2 tablespoons fresh lemon juice
- Salt and black pepper, to taste
- Lemon zest, for garnish (optional)

Instructions:

1. Blanch the Green Beans:

- Bring a large pot of salted water to a boil. Add the haricots verts and cook for 2-3 minutes until they are bright green and crisp-tender. Quickly transfer the green beans to a bowl of ice water to stop the cooking process. Drain and set aside.

2. Toast the Almonds:

- In a large skillet, melt the butter over medium heat. Add the sliced almonds and toast them for 2-3 minutes, stirring frequently, until they become golden brown and fragrant.

3. Add Green Beans:

- Add the blanched haricots verts to the skillet with the toasted almonds. Toss to coat the green beans with the butter and almonds.

4. Season with Lemon Juice:

- Drizzle fresh lemon juice over the green beans and almonds. Season with salt and black pepper to taste. Toss again to combine.

5. Garnish and Serve:

- Optionally, garnish the dish with lemon zest for an extra burst of citrus flavor.

6. Serve Warm:

- Transfer the Haricots Verts Amandine to a serving platter and serve immediately.

Enjoy this elegant and simple French side dish, Haricots Verts Amandine. The combination of crisp-tender green beans, buttery almonds, and zesty lemon creates a delightful medley of flavors and textures. It's a perfect accompaniment to a variety of main dishes.

Provençal Tomato Tart Recipe

Ingredients:

For the Tart Crust:

- 1 1/4 cups all-purpose flour
- 1/2 cup unsalted butter, cold and diced
- 1/4 teaspoon salt
- 3-4 tablespoons ice water

For the Filling:

- 4-5 large tomatoes, sliced
- 1 tablespoon Dijon mustard
- 1 cup Gruyère or Swiss cheese, grated
- 1/4 cup black olives, pitted and sliced
- 2 tablespoons fresh basil, chopped
- 2 tablespoons fresh thyme leaves
- Salt and black pepper, to taste
- Olive oil, for drizzling

Instructions:

1. Prepare the Tart Crust:

- In a food processor, combine the flour, cold diced butter, and salt. Pulse until the mixture resembles coarse crumbs.
- Add ice water, one tablespoon at a time, and pulse until the dough comes together. Be careful not to overmix.
- Form the dough into a disc, wrap it in plastic wrap, and refrigerate for at least 30 minutes.

2. Roll out the Tart Dough:

- Preheat the oven to 375°F (190°C).
- On a lightly floured surface, roll out the chilled tart dough into a circle large enough to fit your tart pan.
- Press the rolled-out dough into a tart pan, trimming any excess. Prick the bottom of the crust with a fork.

3. Pre-bake the Crust:

   - Line the tart crust with parchment paper and fill it with pie weights or dried beans.
   - Pre-bake the crust for about 15 minutes. Remove the parchment and weights, and bake for an additional 5 minutes until the crust is golden brown.

4. Assemble the Tart:

   - Spread a thin layer of Dijon mustard over the bottom of the pre-baked tart crust.
   - Sprinkle half of the grated Gruyère or Swiss cheese over the mustard layer.
   - Arrange the sliced tomatoes over the cheese. Season with salt and black pepper.
   - Sprinkle the remaining cheese over the tomatoes. Scatter sliced black olives on top.

5. Bake the Tart:

   - Bake the tomato tart in the preheated oven for about 25-30 minutes or until the crust is golden brown and the cheese is melted and bubbly.

6. Garnish and Serve:

   - Remove the tart from the oven and sprinkle fresh basil and thyme leaves over the top.
   - Drizzle a bit of olive oil over the tart.
   - Allow the tart to cool slightly before slicing.

7. Serve Warm or at Room Temperature:

   - Serve the Provençal Tomato Tart warm or at room temperature. It's a delightful dish that captures the flavors of Provence.

Enjoy this Provençal Tomato Tart with its vibrant colors, savory flavors, and buttery crust. It makes a beautiful appetizer or a light meal, especially during the summer months when tomatoes are at their peak.

Potato Leek Soup (Vichyssoise) Recipe

Ingredients:

- 3 leeks, white and light green parts only, thoroughly washed and sliced
- 3 large potatoes, peeled and diced
- 1 onion, chopped
- 2 tablespoons unsalted butter
- 4 cups (1 liter) chicken or vegetable broth
- 1 cup (240ml) whole milk
- 1 cup (240ml) heavy cream
- Salt and white pepper, to taste
- Chives, chopped, for garnish (optional)

Instructions:

1. Sauté Vegetables:

- In a large pot, melt the butter over medium heat. Add the chopped leeks, potatoes, and onion. Sauté for about 5-7 minutes until the vegetables are softened but not browned.

2. Add Broth:

- Pour in the chicken or vegetable broth, ensuring that it covers the vegetables. Bring the mixture to a boil, then reduce the heat and let it simmer until the potatoes are tender.

3. Blend the Soup:

- Using an immersion blender, blend the soup until smooth and creamy. If you don't have an immersion blender, carefully transfer the soup in batches to a blender and blend until smooth. Be cautious with hot liquids.

4. Add Milk and Cream:

- Stir in the whole milk and heavy cream. Continue to simmer the soup for an additional 5-7 minutes, allowing the flavors to meld.

5. Season:

- Season the soup with salt and white pepper to taste. Adjust the seasoning as needed.

6. Chill (Optional):

- Vichyssoise is traditionally served chilled. If you prefer a cold soup, allow it to cool to room temperature, then refrigerate for at least 2 hours before serving.

7. Serve:

- Ladle the potato leek soup into bowls. Garnish with chopped chives if desired.

8. Enjoy:

- Enjoy the classic and comforting taste of Potato Leek Soup, also known as Vichyssoise. It's a versatile dish that can be served warm or chilled, making it perfect for any season.

This Potato Leek Soup is a timeless French classic, known for its velvety texture and delicate flavor. Whether served warm on a cool day or chilled during the warmer months, it's a delightful and elegant dish that can be enjoyed year-round.

Lyonnaise Potatoes Recipe

Ingredients:

- 4 large potatoes, peeled and thinly sliced
- 2 large onions, thinly sliced
- 4 tablespoons unsalted butter
- 2 tablespoons olive oil
- 1 teaspoon sugar
- Salt and black pepper, to taste
- Fresh parsley, chopped, for garnish (optional)

Instructions:

1. Slice Potatoes and Onions:

- Peel and thinly slice the potatoes. Also, thinly slice the onions.

2. Sauté Onions:

- In a large skillet, heat 2 tablespoons of butter and 1 tablespoon of olive oil over medium heat. Add the sliced onions and sauté until they become soft and caramelized, about 10-15 minutes.

3. Cook Potatoes:

- In a separate pan, heat the remaining 2 tablespoons of butter and 1 tablespoon of olive oil. Add the thinly sliced potatoes. Cook until the potatoes are golden brown and cooked through, about 10-15 minutes. You may need to do this in batches depending on the size of your pan.

4. Combine Onions and Potatoes:

- Combine the sautéed onions with the cooked potatoes in one of the pans. Sprinkle the sugar over the mixture to aid caramelization. Season with salt and black pepper to taste.

5. Finish Cooking:

- Allow the potatoes and onions to cook together for an additional 5-10 minutes until they are well combined and have a golden color.

6. Garnish and Serve:

- If desired, garnish with chopped fresh parsley for a burst of color and added flavor.

7. Serve Warm:

- Lyonnaise Potatoes are traditionally served warm as a delicious side dish.

8. Enjoy:

- Enjoy the rich and flavorful taste of Lyonnaise Potatoes, a classic French dish that combines the earthiness of potatoes with the sweetness of caramelized onions.

Lyonnaise Potatoes are a delightful accompaniment to a variety of main dishes and add a touch of French culinary elegance to your table.

Pommes Anna (Layered Potatoes) Recipe

Ingredients:

- 4-5 large potatoes, peeled and thinly sliced
- 1/2 cup (1 stick) unsalted butter, melted
- Salt and black pepper, to taste
- Fresh thyme leaves or rosemary sprigs, for garnish (optional)

Instructions:

1. Preheat Oven:

- Preheat your oven to 375°F (190°C).

2. Prepare Potatoes:

- Peel the potatoes and thinly slice them. You can use a mandoline for uniform slices.

3. Brush Baking Dish:

- Brush the bottom and sides of a round baking dish with melted butter.

4. Assemble Layers:

- Arrange a layer of overlapping potato slices in a circular pattern at the bottom of the baking dish. Brush the layer with melted butter and sprinkle with salt and black pepper.
- Repeat the process, layering the potatoes, brushing with butter, and seasoning until you use all the potato slices.

5. Bake:

- Place the baking dish in the preheated oven and bake for approximately 45-55 minutes or until the top is golden brown and the potatoes are tender.

6. Press and Crisp the Top (Optional):

- If desired, you can place a weight on top of the Pommes Anna for the last 10-15 minutes of baking to compress the layers and crisp the top.

7. Garnish:

- Once done, remove from the oven and let it rest for a few minutes. Run a knife around the edges to loosen the Pommes Anna.
- Invert the Pommes Anna onto a serving platter. Garnish with fresh thyme leaves or rosemary sprigs if desired.

8. Serve:

- Slice and serve the Pommes Anna warm, allowing the layers of potatoes to showcase their buttery and crispy goodness.

9. Enjoy:

- Enjoy this classic French dish, Pommes Anna, as a delicious and elegant side that pairs well with a variety of main courses.

Pommes Anna is a simple yet impressive dish that highlights the natural flavors of thinly sliced potatoes cooked to golden perfection. It's a wonderful addition to any special meal or holiday feast.

Grilled Asparagus with Hollandaise Sauce Recipe

Ingredients:

For the Grilled Asparagus:

- 1 bunch of fresh asparagus, tough ends trimmed
- 2 tablespoons olive oil
- Salt and black pepper, to taste

For the Hollandaise Sauce:

- 3 large egg yolks
- 1 tablespoon water
- 1 tablespoon lemon juice
- 1/2 cup (1 stick) unsalted butter, melted
- Pinch of cayenne pepper (optional)
- Salt, to taste
- Chopped fresh chives, for garnish (optional)

Instructions:

1. Grill Asparagus:

- Preheat the grill to medium-high heat.
- Toss the trimmed asparagus with olive oil, salt, and black pepper.
- Grill the asparagus for about 3-5 minutes, turning occasionally, until they are tender and slightly charred. Cooking time may vary based on the thickness of the asparagus.

2. Prepare Hollandaise Sauce:

- In a heatproof bowl, whisk together the egg yolks, water, and lemon juice.
- Place the bowl over a pot of simmering water (double boiler). Ensure that the bottom of the bowl doesn't touch the water.
- Whisk the egg mixture continuously until it thickens and becomes pale in color.
- Slowly drizzle in the melted butter while whisking constantly. Continue whisking until the sauce has a smooth and velvety consistency.
- If desired, add a pinch of cayenne pepper for a hint of heat. Season with salt to taste.

3. Serve:

- Arrange the grilled asparagus on a serving platter.
- Drizzle the Hollandaise sauce generously over the grilled asparagus.
- Garnish with chopped fresh chives if desired.

4. Enjoy:

- Serve the Grilled Asparagus with Hollandaise Sauce immediately while the asparagus is warm and the sauce is silky. Enjoy this classic and indulgent side dish!

Grilled Asparagus with Hollandaise Sauce is a timeless and elegant combination that elevates the natural flavors of asparagus with the richness of a buttery, lemony hollandaise. It's a perfect side dish for special occasions or whenever you want to add a touch of sophistication to your meal.

Fougasse (Provençal Flatbread) Recipe

Ingredients:

For the Dough:

- 3 cups all-purpose flour
- 1 teaspoon salt
- 1 teaspoon sugar
- 1 tablespoon active dry yeast
- 1 cup lukewarm water
- 3 tablespoons olive oil

For Topping (Optional):

- Olive oil
- Herbs (rosemary, thyme, or oregano)
- Coarse sea salt

Instructions:

1. Activate Yeast:

- In a small bowl, combine the lukewarm water, sugar, and active dry yeast. Let it sit for about 5-10 minutes until the mixture becomes frothy.

2. Mix Dough:

- In a large mixing bowl, combine the flour and salt. Make a well in the center and pour in the activated yeast mixture and olive oil.
- Mix until a dough forms. Knead the dough on a floured surface for about 5-7 minutes until it becomes smooth and elastic.

3. First Rise:

- Place the dough in a lightly oiled bowl, cover with a kitchen towel, and let it rise in a warm place for 1-2 hours or until it has doubled in size.

4. Shape Fougasse:

- Preheat your oven to 400°F (200°C). Line a baking sheet with parchment paper.
- Punch down the risen dough and transfer it to a floured surface. Divide it in half.
- Roll out each half into an oval or leaf shape. Use a knife or scissors to make cuts in the dough to create a leaf or wheat stalk pattern. Pull the cut sections slightly apart.

5. Second Rise:

- Place the shaped fougasse on the prepared baking sheet. Cover it with a kitchen towel and let it rise for another 30-45 minutes.

6. Optional Toppings:

- Brush the surface of the fougasse with olive oil. Sprinkle herbs and coarse sea salt on top.

7. Bake:

- Bake in the preheated oven for 15-20 minutes or until the fougasse is golden brown and sounds hollow when tapped on the bottom.

8. Cool and Serve:

- Allow the fougasse to cool on a wire rack before serving.

9. Enjoy:

- Serve the Fougasse as a delicious accompaniment to soups, salads, or charcuterie. Enjoy the crusty exterior and soft interior of this traditional Provençal flatbread.

Fougasse is not only a delightful bread to enjoy with meals but also a beautiful centerpiece with its intricate leaf or wheat stalk pattern. Its rustic charm and wonderful flavor make it a perfect addition to your bread-baking repertoire.

Soufflé au Fromage (Cheese Soufflé) Recipe

Ingredients:

- 3 tablespoons unsalted butter, plus extra for greasing
- 3 tablespoons all-purpose flour
- 1 cup whole milk, warmed
- 1/2 teaspoon Dijon mustard
- Salt and black pepper, to taste
- Pinch of cayenne pepper (optional)
- 4 large eggs, separated
- 1 1/4 cups grated Gruyère or Swiss cheese
- Parmesan cheese, for coating the soufflé dish

Instructions:

1. Preheat Oven:

   - Preheat your oven to 375°F (190°C). Butter and coat a soufflé dish with Parmesan cheese.

2. Make the Roux:

   - In a saucepan, melt 3 tablespoons of butter over medium heat. Add the flour and whisk continuously to create a smooth roux. Cook for a couple of minutes to remove the raw taste of the flour.

3. Create Béchamel Sauce:

   - Gradually whisk in the warm milk to the roux, making sure there are no lumps. Continue to cook and whisk until the mixture thickens to a smooth béchamel sauce.

4. Season the Sauce:

   - Stir in Dijon mustard, salt, black pepper, and cayenne pepper (if using). Adjust the seasoning to your taste.

5. Add Egg Yolks and Cheese:

- Remove the saucepan from the heat. Quickly whisk in the egg yolks one at a time. Stir in the grated Gruyère or Swiss cheese until it melts into the sauce.

6. Beat Egg Whites:

- In a clean, dry bowl, beat the egg whites with a pinch of salt until stiff peaks form.

7. Fold in Egg Whites:

- Gently fold one-third of the beaten egg whites into the cheese mixture to lighten it. Then, carefully fold in the remaining egg whites until just combined. Be gentle to preserve the volume of the egg whites.

8. Fill Soufflé Dish:

- Pour the soufflé mixture into the prepared dish, leveling the top with a spatula.

9. Bake:

- Place the soufflé dish in the preheated oven and bake for 25-30 minutes or until the soufflé is puffed, golden brown, and set in the center.

10. Serve Immediately:

- Serve the Cheese Soufflé immediately, as it will begin to deflate after coming out of the oven.

11. Enjoy:

- Enjoy the light and airy texture of this classic Cheese Soufflé. Serve it as a delightful and elegant dish for a special occasion or as a comforting treat for a cozy meal.

A well-executed Cheese Soufflé is a culinary triumph, and making one at home is both rewarding and impressive. The key is to work quickly and confidently, and you'll be rewarded with a deliciously airy and cheesy masterpiece.

Breads:

Baguette Recipe

Ingredients:

- 4 cups all-purpose flour
- 1 tablespoon active dry yeast
- 1 1/2 teaspoons salt
- 1 1/2 cups warm water (110°F/43°C)
- Cornmeal (for dusting)

Instructions:

1. Activate Yeast:

- In a small bowl, combine the warm water and active dry yeast. Let it sit for 5-10 minutes until the mixture becomes frothy.

2. Mix Dough:

- In a large mixing bowl, combine the flour and salt. Make a well in the center and pour in the activated yeast mixture.
- Stir the mixture with a wooden spoon until it comes together to form a dough.

3. Knead Dough:

- Transfer the dough to a floured surface and knead for about 10 minutes until it becomes smooth and elastic. You can also use a stand mixer with a dough hook for this step.

4. First Rise:

- Place the kneaded dough in a lightly oiled bowl, cover it with a kitchen towel, and let it rise in a warm place for 1-2 hours or until it has doubled in size.

5. Shape the Baguette:

- Punch down the risen dough and transfer it to a floured surface. Divide it into two equal portions.

- Roll each portion into a rectangle, then tightly roll it up from the long side to form a baguette shape.
- Place the shaped baguettes on a parchment paper-lined or lightly greased baking sheet that has been dusted with cornmeal.

6. Second Rise:

- Cover the shaped baguettes with a kitchen towel and let them rise for another 30-45 minutes.

7. Preheat Oven:

- Preheat your oven to 450°F (230°C).

8. Score the Baguettes:

- Using a sharp knife or razor blade, make diagonal slashes (score) on the top of each baguette. This helps the bread expand while baking.

9. Bake:

- Place the baking sheet in the preheated oven and bake for 20-25 minutes or until the baguettes are golden brown and have a hollow sound when tapped on the bottom.

10. Cool:

- Allow the baguettes to cool on a wire rack before slicing.

11. Enjoy:

- Enjoy your homemade baguette with your favorite toppings, or use it to make sandwiches. The crusty exterior and soft interior make it perfect for various culinary creations.

Making a baguette at home allows you to savor the irresistible aroma and taste of freshly baked bread. With a crisp crust and tender crumb, this classic French bread is a delightful addition to any meal.

Pain de Campagne (Country Bread) Recipe

Ingredients:

For the Poolish (Starter):

- 1 cup all-purpose flour
- 1 cup lukewarm water
- 1/4 teaspoon active dry yeast

For the Bread Dough:

- 2 1/2 cups bread flour
- 1 cup whole wheat flour
- 1 1/2 teaspoons salt
- 1 teaspoon active dry yeast
- 1 1/2 cups lukewarm water
- All of the prepared poolish

Instructions:

1. Prepare the Poolish:

- In a bowl, combine 1 cup of all-purpose flour, 1 cup of lukewarm water, and 1/4 teaspoon of active dry yeast. Mix until well combined.
- Cover the bowl with plastic wrap and let the poolish ferment at room temperature for about 12-16 hours or until it becomes bubbly and has a pleasant aroma.

2. Mix the Bread Dough:

- In a large mixing bowl, combine the bread flour, whole wheat flour, salt, and 1 teaspoon of active dry yeast.
- Make a well in the center and add the lukewarm water. Pour in all of the prepared poolish.
- Mix the ingredients until a shaggy dough forms.

3. Knead the Dough:

- Transfer the dough to a floured surface and knead for about 10-15 minutes until it becomes smooth and elastic. You can also use a stand mixer with a dough hook for this step.

4. First Rise:

    - Place the kneaded dough in a lightly oiled bowl, cover it with a kitchen towel, and let it rise in a warm place for 1-2 hours or until it has doubled in size.

5. Shape the Bread:

    - Turn the risen dough onto a floured surface and shape it into a round or oval loaf.
    - Place the shaped dough on a parchment paper-lined or lightly greased baking sheet.

6. Second Rise:

    - Cover the shaped loaf with a kitchen towel and let it rise for another 1-2 hours or until it has doubled in size.

7. Preheat Oven:

    - Preheat your oven to 450°F (230°C).

8. Score the Bread:

    - Using a sharp knife or razor blade, make shallow slashes (score) on the top of the bread. This helps the bread expand while baking.

9. Bake:

    - Place the baking sheet in the preheated oven and bake for 25-30 minutes or until the bread is golden brown and has a hollow sound when tapped on the bottom.

10. Cool:

    - Allow the country bread to cool on a wire rack before slicing.

11. Enjoy:

- Savor the rustic flavor and hearty texture of your homemade Pain de Campagne. This country bread is perfect for sandwiches, toasts, or simply enjoyed with your favorite spread.

Pain de Campagne, with its combination of all-purpose and whole wheat flours, captures the essence of rustic country-style bread. The poolish adds depth of flavor and a beautiful crumb, making this homemade loaf a wholesome and satisfying treat.

Pain Complet (Whole Wheat Bread) Recipe

Ingredients:

- 2 1/2 cups whole wheat flour
- 1 1/2 cups all-purpose flour
- 1 tablespoon active dry yeast
- 1 1/2 teaspoons salt
- 1 tablespoon honey or maple syrup
- 2 tablespoons olive oil or vegetable oil
- 1 1/4 cups lukewarm water

Instructions:

1. Activate Yeast:

- In a small bowl, combine the lukewarm water, honey (or maple syrup), and active dry yeast. Let it sit for 5-10 minutes until the mixture becomes frothy.

2. Mix the Dough:

- In a large mixing bowl, combine the whole wheat flour, all-purpose flour, and salt.
- Create a well in the center of the flour mixture and pour in the activated yeast mixture and olive oil.
- Stir the ingredients until a dough forms.

3. Knead the Dough:

- Transfer the dough to a floured surface and knead for about 10-15 minutes until it becomes smooth and elastic. You can also use a stand mixer with a dough hook for this step.

4. First Rise:

- Place the kneaded dough in a lightly oiled bowl, cover it with a kitchen towel, and let it rise in a warm place for 1-2 hours or until it has doubled in size.

5. Shape the Bread:

- Turn the risen dough onto a floured surface and shape it into a loaf.

- Place the shaped dough in a greased or parchment paper-lined loaf pan.

6. Second Rise:

    - Cover the loaf with a kitchen towel and let it rise for another 1-2 hours or until it has doubled in size.

7. Preheat Oven:

    - Preheat your oven to 375°F (190°C).

8. Bake:

    - Place the loaf pan in the preheated oven and bake for 25-30 minutes or until the bread is golden brown and sounds hollow when tapped on the bottom.

9. Cool:

    - Allow the whole wheat bread to cool in the pan for a few minutes, then transfer it to a wire rack to cool completely.

10. Slice and Enjoy:

    - Once cooled, slice the Pain Complet and enjoy it with your favorite spreads or as a wholesome accompaniment to meals.

This Pain Complet (Whole Wheat Bread) recipe provides a nutritious and flavorful loaf that's perfect for those who prefer the heartiness of whole wheat. The addition of honey or maple syrup adds a touch of sweetness, making it a versatile bread suitable for various occasions.

Pain Complet (Whole Wheat Bread) Recipe

Ingredients:

- 2 1/2 cups whole wheat flour
- 1 1/2 cups all-purpose flour
- 1 tablespoon active dry yeast
- 1 1/2 teaspoons salt
- 1 tablespoon honey or maple syrup
- 2 tablespoons olive oil or vegetable oil
- 1 1/4 cups lukewarm water

Instructions:

1. Activate Yeast:

- In a small bowl, combine the lukewarm water, honey (or maple syrup), and active dry yeast. Let it sit for 5-10 minutes until the mixture becomes frothy.

2. Mix the Dough:

- In a large mixing bowl, combine the whole wheat flour, all-purpose flour, and salt.
- Create a well in the center of the flour mixture and pour in the activated yeast mixture and olive oil.
- Stir the ingredients until a dough forms.

3. Knead the Dough:

- Transfer the dough to a floured surface and knead for about 10-15 minutes until it becomes smooth and elastic. You can also use a stand mixer with a dough hook for this step.

4. First Rise:

- Place the kneaded dough in a lightly oiled bowl, cover it with a kitchen towel, and let it rise in a warm place for 1-2 hours or until it has doubled in size.

5. Shape the Bread:

- Turn the risen dough onto a floured surface and shape it into a loaf.

- Place the shaped dough in a greased or parchment paper-lined loaf pan.

6. Second Rise:

    - Cover the loaf with a kitchen towel and let it rise for another 1-2 hours or until it has doubled in size.

7. Preheat Oven:

    - Preheat your oven to 375°F (190°C).

8. Bake:

    - Place the loaf pan in the preheated oven and bake for 25-30 minutes or until the bread is golden brown and sounds hollow when tapped on the bottom.

9. Cool:

    - Allow the whole wheat bread to cool in the pan for a few minutes, then transfer it to a wire rack to cool completely.

10. Slice and Enjoy:

    - Once cooled, slice the Pain Complet and enjoy it with your favorite spreads or as a wholesome accompaniment to meals.

This Pain Complet (Whole Wheat Bread) recipe provides a nutritious and flavorful loaf that's perfect for those who prefer the heartiness of whole wheat. The addition of honey or maple syrup adds a touch of sweetness, making it a versatile bread suitable for various occasions.

Pain Poilâne (Sourdough Bread) Recipe

Ingredients:

For the Sourdough Starter:

- 1/2 cup active sourdough starter
- 1 cup all-purpose flour
- 1/2 cup lukewarm water

For the Bread Dough:

- 3 cups bread flour
- 1 cup whole wheat flour
- 1 1/2 teaspoons salt
- 1 1/4 cups lukewarm water
- 1/4 cup honey or maple syrup (optional, for a touch of sweetness)

Instructions:

1. Prepare the Sourdough Starter:

- In a bowl, mix 1/2 cup active sourdough starter with 1 cup all-purpose flour and 1/2 cup lukewarm water. Stir well until it forms a thick, paste-like consistency.
- Cover the bowl loosely with a cloth and let it sit in a warm place for 4-8 hours or overnight until it becomes bubbly and active.

2. Mix the Bread Dough:

- In a large mixing bowl, combine the bread flour, whole wheat flour, and salt.
- Create a well in the center and add the lukewarm water, honey (if using), and the prepared sourdough starter.
- Mix the ingredients until a shaggy dough forms.

3. Knead the Dough:

- Transfer the dough to a floured surface and knead for about 10-15 minutes until it becomes smooth and elastic. You can also use a stand mixer with a dough hook for this step.

4. First Rise:

- Place the kneaded dough in a lightly oiled bowl, cover it with a kitchen towel, and let it rise in a warm place for 4-8 hours or until it has doubled in size. This is the bulk fermentation phase.

5. Shape the Bread:

- Turn the risen dough onto a floured surface and shape it into a round or oval loaf.
- Place the shaped dough in a floured proofing basket or on a parchment paper-lined baking sheet.

6. Second Rise (Proofing):

- Cover the shaped loaf with a kitchen towel and let it rise for another 4-8 hours or until it has increased in size and passes the poke test. The poke test is done by gently pressing your finger into the dough; if the indentation slowly fills back, it's ready.

7. Preheat Oven:

- Preheat your oven to 450°F (230°C). If you have a baking stone, place it in the oven during the preheating.

8. Score the Bread:

- Just before baking, score the top of the loaf with a sharp knife or razor blade. This helps the bread expand while baking.

9. Bake:

- If using a baking stone, carefully transfer the shaped dough onto the preheated stone or bake it on a parchment paper-lined baking sheet.
- Bake for 30-40 minutes or until the bread is golden brown and has a hollow sound when tapped on the bottom.

10. Cool:

- Allow the Pain Poilâne to cool on a wire rack before slicing.

11. Enjoy:

    - Slice and enjoy your homemade Pain Poilâne, a classic sourdough bread with a distinct flavor and chewy texture.

Pain Poilâne, known for its hearty texture and rich flavor, is a wonderful sourdough bread that can be a centerpiece for your meals or a delightful accompaniment to a variety of dishes. This recipe allows you to capture the essence of this iconic French bread in your own kitchen.

Pain d'Épices (Spice Bread) Recipe

Ingredients:

- 1 1/2 cups all-purpose flour
- 1/2 cup whole wheat flour
- 1 teaspoon baking powder
- 1/2 teaspoon baking soda
- 1/2 teaspoon salt
- 2 teaspoons ground cinnamon
- 1 teaspoon ground ginger
- 1/2 teaspoon ground nutmeg
- 1/4 teaspoon ground cloves
- 1/4 teaspoon ground allspice
- 1/2 cup unsalted butter, softened
- 1/2 cup honey
- 1/2 cup molasses
- 2 large eggs
- 1 cup buttermilk

Instructions:

1. Preheat Oven:

    - Preheat your oven to 350°F (175°C). Grease and flour a loaf pan.

2. Mix Dry Ingredients:

    - In a medium bowl, whisk together the all-purpose flour, whole wheat flour, baking powder, baking soda, salt, cinnamon, ginger, nutmeg, cloves, and allspice. Set aside.

3. Cream Butter and Sweeteners:

    - In a large bowl, cream together the softened butter, honey, and molasses until light and fluffy.

4. Add Eggs:

    - Add the eggs one at a time, beating well after each addition.

5. Alternate Dry Ingredients and Buttermilk:

- Gradually add the dry ingredients to the wet ingredients, alternating with the buttermilk. Begin and end with the dry ingredients.

6. Mix Until Just Combined:

- Mix the batter until just combined. Be careful not to overmix.

7. Pour into Pan:

- Pour the batter into the prepared loaf pan, spreading it evenly.

8. Bake:

- Bake in the preheated oven for 50-60 minutes or until a toothpick inserted into the center comes out clean.

9. Cool:

- Allow the spice bread to cool in the pan for about 10 minutes, then transfer it to a wire rack to cool completely.

10. Slice and Enjoy:

- Once cooled, slice the Pain d'Épices and enjoy the rich, spiced flavors.

11. Optional: Glaze (Optional):

- If desired, you can glaze the spice bread with a simple mixture of powdered sugar and milk. Drizzle the glaze over the cooled bread.

12. Serve:

- Serve the Pain d'Épices with a cup of tea or coffee for a delightful treat.

This Pain d'Épices recipe brings together a medley of warm spices, honey, and molasses to create a flavorful and aromatic bread. Whether enjoyed on its own or with a spread of butter, this spice bread is a comforting and festive addition to your baking repertoire.

Desserts:

Tarte Tatin Recipe

Ingredients:

For the Pastry:

- 1 1/4 cups all-purpose flour
- 1/2 cup unsalted butter, cold and cut into small pieces
- 1/4 cup granulated sugar
- 1/4 teaspoon salt
- 2-3 tablespoons ice water

For the Tarte Tatin:

- 6-7 large apples (such as Granny Smith), peeled, cored, and halved
- 1 cup granulated sugar
- 1/2 cup unsalted butter
- 1 teaspoon vanilla extract
- Pastry dough (from the above ingredients)

Instructions:

1. Prepare the Pastry Dough:

- In a food processor, combine the flour, cold butter, sugar, and salt. Pulse until the mixture resembles coarse crumbs.
- Add ice water, one tablespoon at a time, and pulse until the dough comes together. Be careful not to overmix.
- Gather the dough into a ball, flatten it into a disk, wrap it in plastic wrap, and refrigerate for at least 1 hour.

2. Preheat Oven:

- Preheat your oven to 375°F (190°C).

3. Make the Caramel:

- In a 9 or 10-inch ovenproof skillet or Tatin dish, melt the butter over medium heat. Add the sugar and cook, stirring occasionally, until the sugar dissolves and turns into a golden caramel.

4. Arrange Apples:

    - Arrange the apple halves, rounded side down, in a circular pattern over the caramel. Fill the entire bottom of the skillet with apples.

5. Cook the Apples:

    - Cook the apples over medium heat for about 15-20 minutes or until they are tender and the caramel has thickened.

6. Add Vanilla Extract:

    - Stir in the vanilla extract.

7. Roll Out Pastry:

    - On a floured surface, roll out the chilled pastry dough to fit the size of the skillet.

8. Cover Apples with Pastry:

    - Place the rolled-out pastry over the cooked apples, tucking the edges down around the apples.

9. Bake:

    - Bake in the preheated oven for 25-30 minutes or until the pastry is golden brown.

10. Cool and Invert:

    - Allow the Tarte Tatin to cool for a few minutes before inverting it onto a serving platter. Be careful, as the caramel will be hot.

11. Serve:

    - Serve the Tarte Tatin warm, either on its own or with a dollop of whipped cream or a scoop of vanilla ice cream.

12. Enjoy:

    - Enjoy the delicious upside-down caramelized apple goodness of Tarte Tatin!

Tarte Tatin is a classic French dessert known for its caramelized apples and buttery pastry. This recipe delivers a delightful combination of sweet, sticky caramel and tender apples encased in a flaky crust. Serve it as a stunning and delicious finale to any meal.

Crème Brûlée Recipe

Ingredients:

- 2 cups heavy cream
- 1 vanilla bean or 1 tablespoon vanilla extract
- 5 large egg yolks
- 1/2 cup granulated sugar, plus extra for caramelizing

Instructions:

1. Preheat Oven:

- Preheat your oven to 325°F (160°C). Place ramekins in a baking dish that will accommodate them.

2. Heat Cream:

- In a saucepan, heat the heavy cream over medium heat until it is hot but not boiling. If using a vanilla bean, split it lengthwise, scrape the seeds into the cream, and add the vanilla bean pod. If using vanilla extract, add it directly to the cream. Remove from heat and let it steep for about 15 minutes.

3. Whisk Egg Yolks and Sugar:

- In a bowl, whisk together the egg yolks and sugar until the mixture is pale and slightly thickened.

4. Temper the Eggs:

- Slowly pour a small amount of the hot cream into the egg yolk mixture, whisking constantly to temper the eggs. Gradually add the remaining cream, continuing to whisk.

5. Strain the Mixture:

- Strain the custard mixture through a fine-mesh sieve into a bowl to remove any cooked egg bits and the vanilla bean pod if used.

6. Fill Ramekins:

- Pour the custard mixture into the prepared ramekins.

7. Create a Water Bath:

    - Place the baking dish with the filled ramekins in the preheated oven. Carefully pour hot water into the baking dish to create a water bath that surrounds the ramekins.

8. Bake:

    - Bake for about 35-40 minutes or until the edges are set but the center still jiggles slightly.

9. Chill:

    - Remove the ramekins from the water bath and let them cool to room temperature. Then, cover and refrigerate for at least 2 hours or overnight.

10. Caramelize the Sugar:

    - Just before serving, sprinkle a thin, even layer of granulated sugar over the chilled custard. Use a kitchen torch to caramelize the sugar until it forms a golden-brown crust.

11. Serve:

    - Allow the Crème Brûlée to sit for a minute to let the caramelized sugar harden. Serve and enjoy!

Crème Brûlée, with its smooth and creamy custard base and the satisfying crack of caramelized sugar on top, is a classic French dessert. It's elegant and delightful, making it a perfect choice for special occasions or any time you crave a luxurious treat.

Profiteroles with Chocolate Sauce Recipe

Ingredients:

For the Profiteroles:

- 1 cup water
- 1/2 cup unsalted butter
- 1 cup all-purpose flour
- 4 large eggs

For the Whipped Cream Filling:

- 2 cups heavy cream
- 1/4 cup powdered sugar
- 1 teaspoon vanilla extract

For the Chocolate Sauce:

- 6 ounces semisweet or bittersweet chocolate, chopped
- 1 cup heavy cream
- 2 tablespoons unsalted butter
- 2 tablespoons sugar
- 1 teaspoon vanilla extract

Instructions:

For the Profiteroles:

1. Preheat Oven:

- Preheat your oven to 425°F (220°C). Line a baking sheet with parchment paper.

2. Make Choux Pastry:

- In a saucepan, combine water and butter over medium heat until the butter melts. Bring the mixture to a boil, then reduce the heat to low and add the flour all at once. Stir vigorously until the mixture forms a ball and pulls away from the sides of the pan.
- Remove from heat and let it cool for a couple of minutes.

3. Add Eggs:

- Add the eggs one at a time, beating well after each addition. The dough should be smooth and shiny.

4. Pipe Dough:

- Transfer the dough to a piping bag fitted with a large round tip. Pipe small mounds (about 1.5 inches in diameter) onto the prepared baking sheet, leaving space between each.

5. Bake:

- Bake in the preheated oven for 15-20 minutes or until the profiteroles are puffed and golden brown. Reduce the oven temperature to 375°F (190°C) and bake for an additional 10-15 minutes to ensure they are cooked through. Let them cool completely.

For the Whipped Cream Filling:

1. Whip Cream:

- In a large bowl, whip the heavy cream, powdered sugar, and vanilla extract until stiff peaks form.

2. Fill Profiteroles:

- Cut the profiteroles in half horizontally and fill each one with a generous amount of whipped cream.

For the Chocolate Sauce:

1. Melt Chocolate:

- In a heatproof bowl, melt the chopped chocolate over a double boiler or in the microwave.

2. Heat Cream:

- In a small saucepan, heat the heavy cream, butter, and sugar over medium heat until it just starts to simmer. Remove from heat.

3. Combine:

- Pour the hot cream mixture over the melted chocolate. Let it sit for a minute, then stir until smooth and well combined. Add vanilla extract and stir again.

4. Serve:

- Drizzle the warm chocolate sauce over the filled profiteroles.

5. Enjoy:

- Serve the Profiteroles with Chocolate Sauce immediately, and enjoy the decadent combination of crispy choux pastry, luscious whipped cream, and rich chocolate sauce.

Profiteroles with Chocolate Sauce make for a delightful and elegant dessert that's sure to impress. The light and airy choux pastry, paired with sweet whipped cream and a velvety chocolate sauce, create a perfect harmony of flavors and textures.

Éclairs Recipe

Ingredients:

For the Choux Pastry:

- 1/2 cup unsalted butter
- 1 cup water
- 1 cup all-purpose flour
- 1/4 teaspoon salt
- 4 large eggs

For the Pastry Cream Filling:

- 2 cups whole milk
- 1/2 cup granulated sugar
- 1/4 cup cornstarch
- 4 large egg yolks
- 2 teaspoons vanilla extract

For the Chocolate Glaze:

- 4 ounces semisweet or bittersweet chocolate, chopped
- 1/2 cup heavy cream
- 2 tablespoons unsalted butter
- 2 tablespoons corn syrup (optional, for shine)

Instructions:

For the Choux Pastry:

1. Preheat Oven:

- Preheat your oven to 400°F (200°C). Line a baking sheet with parchment paper.

2. Make Choux Dough:

- In a saucepan, combine butter and water over medium heat until the butter is melted. Bring the mixture to a boil. Remove from heat and add the flour and salt all at once. Stir vigorously until the mixture forms a ball.

3. Add Eggs:

- Let the dough cool for a couple of minutes. Add the eggs one at a time, beating well after each addition. The dough should be smooth and shiny.

4. Pipe Dough:

- Transfer the choux pastry dough to a piping bag fitted with a large round tip. Pipe the dough onto the prepared baking sheet into 4-inch long strips, leaving space between each.

5. Bake:

- Bake in the preheated oven for 15-20 minutes or until the éclairs are puffed and golden brown. Reduce the oven temperature to 350°F (180°C) and bake for an additional 10-15 minutes to ensure they are cooked through. Let them cool completely.

For the Pastry Cream Filling:

1. Heat Milk:

- In a saucepan, heat the milk until it is just about to boil. Remove from heat.

2. Mix Sugar and Egg Yolks:

- In a bowl, whisk together sugar, cornstarch, and egg yolks until well combined.

3. Temper Eggs:

- Slowly pour a small amount of the hot milk into the egg mixture, whisking constantly to temper the eggs. Gradually add the remaining hot milk, continuing to whisk.

4. Cook Mixture:

- Pour the mixture back into the saucepan and cook over medium heat, stirring constantly, until it thickens to a pudding-like consistency.

5. Add Vanilla:

- Remove from heat and stir in the vanilla extract. Let the pastry cream cool.

For the Chocolate Glaze:

1. Melt Chocolate:

- In a heatproof bowl, melt the chopped chocolate over a double boiler or in the microwave.

2. Heat Cream:

- In a small saucepan, heat the heavy cream until it just starts to simmer. Remove from heat.

3. Combine:

- Pour the hot cream over the melted chocolate. Let it sit for a minute, then stir until smooth and well combined. Add butter and corn syrup (if using) and stir again.

4. Assemble Éclairs:

- Cut the cooled éclairs in half horizontally. Fill each éclair with the cooled pastry cream.
- Dip the top of each filled éclair into the warm chocolate glaze, allowing any excess to drip off.

5. Chill and Serve:

- Place the assembled éclairs in the refrigerator to allow the chocolate glaze to set.

6. Enjoy:

- Serve the chilled éclairs and enjoy this classic French pastry!

Éclairs are a delightful French pastry with a crisp choux shell filled with creamy pastry cream and topped with a glossy chocolate glaze. This homemade éclairs recipe will surely impress with its combination of textures and flavors.

Madeleines Recipe

Ingredients:

- 2/3 cup unsalted butter, melted and cooled
- 1 cup all-purpose flour
- 1/2 teaspoon baking powder
- 1/4 teaspoon salt
- 3 large eggs
- 1 teaspoon vanilla extract
- 2/3 cup granulated sugar
- Zest of 1 lemon (optional, for flavor)

Instructions:

1. Preheat Oven and Prepare Madeleine Pans:

- Preheat your oven to 375°F (190°C). Grease and flour your madeleine pans.

2. Melt Butter:

- Melt the butter in a saucepan or microwave, then let it cool to room temperature.

3. Sift Dry Ingredients:

- In a bowl, sift together the flour, baking powder, and salt. Set aside.

4. Beat Eggs and Sugar:

- In a separate bowl, beat the eggs, granulated sugar, and vanilla extract until the mixture is thick and pale.

5. Add Dry Ingredients:

- Gradually fold in the sifted dry ingredients into the egg and sugar mixture. Be gentle to maintain the airiness.

6. Add Melted Butter:

- Add the cooled melted butter to the batter and fold until well combined. If desired, add the lemon zest for extra flavor.

7. Chill Batter:

- Cover the bowl with plastic wrap and chill the batter in the refrigerator for at least 30 minutes. This helps the madeleines achieve their characteristic hump.

8. Fill Madeleine Pans:

- Spoon the chilled batter into the prepared madeleine pans, filling each shell about 3/4 full.

9. Bake:

- Bake in the preheated oven for 10-12 minutes or until the madeleines are golden around the edges and spring back when lightly pressed in the center.

10. Cool:

- Remove the madeleines from the pans and let them cool on a wire rack.

11. Optional: Dust with Powdered Sugar:

- Once cooled, you can dust the madeleines with powdered sugar for a finishing touch.

12. Serve and Enjoy:

- Serve the madeleines with your favorite hot beverage and enjoy these delicate and classic French treats.

Madeleines are small, shell-shaped sponge cakes with a slightly crispy exterior and a soft, moist interior. They are a delightful accompaniment to tea or coffee, and their charming shape makes them an elegant addition to any dessert table.

Charlotte au Chocolat Recipe

Ingredients:

For the Chocolate Mousse:

- 8 ounces (about 225g) bittersweet chocolate, chopped
- 1 1/2 cups heavy cream
- 1/4 cup granulated sugar
- 4 large egg yolks

For the Chocolate Ladyfingers:

- 2/3 cup all-purpose flour
- 1/3 cup unsweetened cocoa powder
- 4 large eggs, separated
- 1/2 cup granulated sugar
- 1 teaspoon vanilla extract
- Pinch of salt

For the Chocolate Ganache:

- 1/2 cup heavy cream
- 4 ounces (about 115g) bittersweet chocolate, chopped

Instructions:

For the Chocolate Mousse:

1. Melt Chocolate:

- Place the chopped chocolate in a heatproof bowl. In a saucepan, heat 1/2 cup of heavy cream until it simmers. Pour the hot cream over the chocolate and let it sit for a minute. Stir until smooth and let it cool slightly.

2. Whip Cream:

- In a separate bowl, whip the remaining 1 cup of heavy cream with sugar until stiff peaks form.

3. Combine:

- Gently fold the whipped cream into the melted chocolate until well combined.

4. Temper Egg Yolks:

- In another bowl, whisk the egg yolks. Slowly add a small amount of the chocolate mixture to the yolks, whisking constantly to temper the eggs.

5. Combine and Chill:

- Gradually add the tempered egg yolk mixture back into the chocolate mousse, folding gently. Chill the chocolate mousse in the refrigerator while you prepare the ladyfingers.

For the Chocolate Ladyfingers:

1. Preheat Oven:

- Preheat your oven to 350°F (175°C). Line a baking sheet with parchment paper.

2. Sift Dry Ingredients:

- In a bowl, sift together the flour and cocoa powder.

3. Whip Egg Whites:

- In a clean, dry bowl, whip the egg whites with a pinch of salt until soft peaks form. Gradually add sugar and continue whipping until stiff peaks form.

4. Combine Batter:

- Gently fold the sifted dry ingredients into the whipped egg whites.

5. Add Vanilla:

- Stir in the vanilla extract.

6. Pipe Ladyfingers:

- Transfer the batter to a piping bag fitted with a round tip. Pipe the ladyfingers onto the prepared baking sheet.

7. Bake:

    - Bake in the preheated oven for about 10-12 minutes or until the ladyfingers are firm and spring back when touched.

For the Chocolate Ganache:

1. Heat Cream:

    - In a saucepan, heat the cream until it just starts to simmer.

2. Melt Chocolate:

    - Place the chopped chocolate in a heatproof bowl. Pour the hot cream over the chocolate and let it sit for a minute. Stir until smooth.

Assembly:

1. Line Mold:

    - Line the sides of a Charlotte mold or a springform pan with the chocolate ladyfingers, placing them vertically.

2. Fill with Mousse:

    - Pour the chocolate mousse into the center of the mold, smoothing the top with a spatula.

3. Chill:

    - Chill the Charlotte au Chocolat in the refrigerator for at least 4 hours or overnight to set.

4. Ganache Topping:

    - Pour the chocolate ganache over the top of the chilled Charlotte, spreading it evenly.

5. Chill Again:

- Chill for an additional hour to set the ganache.

6. Serve and Enjoy:

- Slice and serve the Charlotte au Chocolat, enjoying the layers of rich chocolate mousse and chocolate ladyfingers.

This Charlotte au Chocolat is a luxurious French dessert featuring layers of velvety chocolate mousse and delicate chocolate ladyfingers. It's an elegant and indulgent treat perfect for special occasions.

Macarons Recipe

Ingredients:

For the Macaron Shells:

- 1 cup (100g) almond flour
- 1 3/4 cups (210g) powdered sugar
- 3 large egg whites, at room temperature
- 1/4 cup (50g) granulated sugar
- Gel food coloring (optional)

For the Filling:

- 1/2 cup (120g) unsalted butter, softened
- 1 cup (120g) powdered sugar
- 1-2 teaspoons vanilla extract
- Food coloring or flavoring (optional)

Instructions:

For the Macaron Shells:

1. Prepare Baking Sheets:

- Line two baking sheets with parchment paper or silicone baking mats.

2. Sift Dry Ingredients:

- In a bowl, sift together almond flour and powdered sugar. Discard any larger almond pieces left in the sieve.

3. Whip Egg Whites:

- In a clean, dry bowl, beat the egg whites until foamy. Gradually add granulated sugar while continuing to beat. Beat until stiff peaks form. If desired, add gel food coloring at this stage.

4. Fold Dry Ingredients:

- Gently fold the sifted almond flour and powdered sugar into the beaten egg whites. Be careful not to deflate the egg whites.

5. Pipe Macarons:

- Transfer the batter to a piping bag fitted with a round tip. Pipe small rounds onto the prepared baking sheets. The rounds should be about 1.5 inches in diameter.

6. Resting Time:

- Let the piped macarons sit at room temperature for about 30-60 minutes. This allows them to develop a skin, which helps in creating the characteristic feet.

7. Preheat Oven:

- Preheat your oven to 300°F (150°C).

8. Bake:

- Bake the macarons in the preheated oven for 15-18 minutes, or until they are set and have developed feet. The baking time may vary, so keep an eye on them.

9. Cool:

- Allow the baked macarons to cool completely on the baking sheets before attempting to remove them.

For the Filling:

1. Make Buttercream:

- In a bowl, beat the softened butter until creamy. Gradually add powdered sugar and vanilla extract, continuing to beat until smooth and fluffy. Add food coloring or flavoring if desired.

2. Assemble Macarons:

- Pair up the cooled macaron shells based on similar sizes. Pipe or spread a small amount of filling on one shell and sandwich it with another.

3. Chill:

- Place the assembled macarons in an airtight container and refrigerate for at least 24 hours. This allows the flavors to meld and the texture to improve.

4. Serve and Enjoy:

- Bring the macarons to room temperature before serving. Enjoy these delicate and flavorful French treats!

Macarons are known for their crisp shells and soft, chewy interiors, with a variety of flavors and colors. Mastering the technique may take some practice, but the result is a delightful and elegant treat that's perfect for any occasion.

Cherry Clafoutis Recipe

Ingredients:

- 2 cups fresh cherries, pitted
- 3 large eggs
- 1 cup whole milk
- 1/2 cup all-purpose flour
- 1/2 cup granulated sugar
- 1 teaspoon vanilla extract
- 1/4 teaspoon almond extract (optional)
- A pinch of salt
- Butter, for greasing the baking dish
- Powdered sugar, for dusting (optional)

Instructions:

1. Preheat Oven:

   - Preheat your oven to 350°F (175°C). Grease a baking dish with butter.

2. Prepare Cherries:

   - Wash and pit the cherries. You can leave the pits in for a more authentic clafoutis flavor or remove them.

3. Arrange Cherries:

   - Arrange the pitted cherries in a single layer in the greased baking dish.

4. Make Batter:

   - In a blender, combine eggs, whole milk, flour, granulated sugar, vanilla extract, almond extract (if using), and a pinch of salt. Blend until the mixture is smooth.

5. Pour Batter Over Cherries:

   - Pour the batter over the arranged cherries in the baking dish.

6. Bake:

- Bake in the preheated oven for about 40-45 minutes or until the clafoutis is set and golden brown on top.

7. Cool Slightly:

- Allow the clafoutis to cool slightly before serving. It is normal for it to deflate a bit as it cools.

8. Dust with Powdered Sugar:

- Optionally, dust the clafoutis with powdered sugar before serving for a decorative touch.

9. Serve:

- Serve the cherry clafoutis warm, either as is or with a scoop of vanilla ice cream or a dollop of whipped cream.

10. Enjoy:

- Enjoy this classic French dessert with the juicy bursts of cherries in a tender, custard-like batter.

Note: Traditional clafoutis is made with cherries, but you can experiment with other fruits such as berries, plums, or sliced peaches. Adjust the sugar quantity based on the sweetness of the fruits you choose.

Chocolate Pots de Crème Recipe

Ingredients:

- 2 cups heavy cream
- 4 ounces bittersweet chocolate, finely chopped
- 1 teaspoon vanilla extract
- 1/3 cup granulated sugar
- 6 large egg yolks
- A pinch of salt
- Whipped cream, for garnish (optional)
- Chocolate shavings, for garnish (optional)

Instructions:

1. Preheat Oven:

    - Preheat your oven to 325°F (160°C). Place 6 ramekins or small jars in a baking dish.

2. Heat Cream:

    - In a saucepan, heat the heavy cream over medium heat until it is hot but not boiling.

3. Melt Chocolate:

    - Place the finely chopped bittersweet chocolate in a heatproof bowl. Pour the hot cream over the chocolate and let it sit for a minute to melt. Stir until smooth and well combined.

4. Add Vanilla Extract:

    - Stir in the vanilla extract into the chocolate mixture.

5. Whisk Egg Yolks:

    - In a separate bowl, whisk together the granulated sugar, egg yolks, and a pinch of salt until well combined.

6. Temper Eggs:

   - Gradually add a small amount of the chocolate mixture to the egg yolk mixture, whisking constantly to temper the eggs.

7. Combine Mixtures:

   - Pour the tempered egg yolk mixture back into the chocolate mixture, stirring continuously until well combined.

8. Strain Mixture:

   - Strain the mixture through a fine-mesh sieve into a large jug or bowl to ensure a smooth consistency.

9. Fill Ramekins:

   - Pour the mixture evenly into the prepared ramekins or jars.

10. Create Water Bath:

    - Place the baking dish with the filled ramekins in the oven. Pour hot water into the baking dish, surrounding the ramekins, creating a water bath. The water should come halfway up the sides of the ramekins.

11. Bake:

    - Bake in the preheated oven for about 30-35 minutes or until the pots de crème are set around the edges but slightly wobbly in the center.

12. Chill:

    - Remove the pots de crème from the water bath and let them cool to room temperature. Then, refrigerate them for at least 4 hours or overnight until fully chilled and set.

13. Garnish and Serve:

    - Before serving, you can garnish the pots de crème with a dollop of whipped cream and chocolate shavings if desired.

14. Enjoy:

- Serve and enjoy these rich and silky chocolate pots de crème!

Pots de Crème, meaning "pots of cream" in French, are a delightful and decadent dessert. This chocolate version is a classic, and the silky texture and rich flavor make it a perfect ending to a special meal.

Baba au Rhum Recipe

Ingredients:

For the Baba Dough:

- 2 1/4 teaspoons (1 packet) active dry yeast
- 1/4 cup warm water (about 110°F or 43°C)
- 2 cups all-purpose flour
- 3 tablespoons granulated sugar
- 1/2 teaspoon salt
- 3 large eggs, room temperature
- 1/2 cup unsalted butter, softened

For the Rum Syrup:

- 1 cup water
- 1 cup granulated sugar
- 1 cup dark rum

For Garnish:

- Whipped cream
- Fresh berries or candied fruit (optional)

Instructions:

For the Baba Dough:

1. Activate Yeast:

- In a small bowl, dissolve the active dry yeast in warm water. Let it sit for about 5 minutes until it becomes frothy.

2. Mix Dry Ingredients:

- In a large bowl, combine the flour, sugar, and salt.

3. Add Wet Ingredients:

- Make a well in the center of the dry ingredients. Pour in the activated yeast, eggs, and softened butter.

4. Knead:

- Mix the ingredients until a soft and sticky dough forms. Turn the dough out onto a floured surface and knead for about 10 minutes until it becomes smooth and elastic.

5. First Rise:

- Place the dough in a lightly greased bowl, cover it with a clean kitchen towel, and let it rise in a warm place for 1-2 hours or until it doubles in size.

6. Preheat Oven:

- Preheat your oven to 375°F (190°C).

7. Shape and Bake:

- Punch down the risen dough and shape it into individual rounds or into a large baba mold. Place the shaped dough in a greased baking dish or mold. Bake in the preheated oven for about 20-25 minutes or until golden brown.

For the Rum Syrup:

1. Make Sugar Syrup:

- In a saucepan, combine water and granulated sugar. Bring to a simmer over medium heat, stirring until the sugar is dissolved.

2. Add Rum:

- Remove the saucepan from heat and stir in the dark rum. Let the syrup cool.

Assembly:

1. Soak with Syrup:

- Once the baked baba is out of the oven and still warm, poke it with a skewer or fork to create holes. Pour the cooled rum syrup over the warm baba, allowing it to soak in. Reserve some syrup for serving.

2. Serve:

- Let the baba absorb the syrup for at least 1-2 hours or overnight.

3. Garnish and Serve:

- Before serving, you can garnish the baba with whipped cream and fresh berries or candied fruit if desired. Serve slices of the soaked baba with additional syrup on the side.

4. Enjoy:

- Baba au Rhum is best enjoyed chilled, and the rich, boozy flavor makes it a delightful and indulgent dessert.

Baba au Rhum is a classic French dessert known for its light and airy texture soaked in a rum-infused syrup. It's a perfect treat for those who appreciate a moist and flavorful dessert with a hint of decadence.

Pastries:

Croissants Recipe

Ingredients:

For the Dough:

- 1 1/4 cups (300 ml) whole milk, lukewarm
- 2 tablespoons active dry yeast
- 1/4 cup (50g) granulated sugar
- 3 1/4 cups (400g) all-purpose flour, plus more for rolling
- 1 teaspoon salt
- 1 cup (225g) unsalted butter, cold

For Rolling and Folding:

- Additional flour for dusting
- 1 cup (225g) unsalted butter, chilled

For Egg Wash:

- 1 egg, beaten with a pinch of salt

Instructions:

1. Activate Yeast:

- In a bowl, combine lukewarm milk, active dry yeast, and sugar. Let it sit for 5-10 minutes until it becomes frothy.

2. Prepare Dough:

- In a large mixing bowl, combine the flour and salt. Make a well in the center and pour in the activated yeast mixture. Mix until it forms a dough.

3. Knead Dough:

- Turn the dough onto a floured surface and knead for about 5 minutes until it becomes smooth. Wrap the dough in plastic wrap and refrigerate for 1 hour.

4. Prepare Butter Layer:

- Roll out the chilled butter between two sheets of parchment paper to form a rectangle, roughly 10x7 inches (25x18 cm). Chill the butter layer in the refrigerator.

5. Laminate Dough:

- Roll out the chilled dough on a floured surface into a rectangle, roughly 15x10 inches (38x25 cm). Place the chilled butter layer on two-thirds of the dough, then fold the uncovered third over the butter layer. Fold the other third over the top, creating three layers. This completes one fold. Chill the dough for 30 minutes.

6. Repeat Folds:

- Repeat the rolling and folding process two more times, chilling the dough between each fold. This makes a total of three folds.

7. Final Rest:

- After the final fold, wrap the dough in plastic wrap and refrigerate for at least 1 hour or overnight.

8. Roll and Shape:

- Roll out the chilled dough on a floured surface into a large rectangle, about 1/4 inch (6 mm) thick. Cut the rectangle into triangles, then roll each triangle into a croissant shape, starting from the wider end.

9. Proofing:

- Place the shaped croissants on a baking sheet, leaving space between each. Cover with a kitchen towel and let them proof at room temperature for 1-2 hours or until they double in size.

10. Preheat Oven:

- Preheat your oven to 400°F (200°C).

11. Egg Wash:

- Brush the proofed croissants with the beaten egg wash.

12. Bake:

    - Bake in the preheated oven for 15-20 minutes or until the croissants are golden brown and puffed up.

13. Cool:

    - Allow the baked croissants to cool on a wire rack before serving.

14. Enjoy:

    - Serve these homemade croissants warm, fresh from the oven, and enjoy the buttery, flaky layers!

Making croissants from scratch is a labor of love, but the result is incredibly rewarding. These homemade croissants have a buttery, flaky texture that pairs perfectly with your favorite jams or simply on their own.

Pain au Chocolat Recipe

Ingredients:

For the Dough:

- 1 1/4 cups (300 ml) whole milk, lukewarm
- 2 tablespoons active dry yeast
- 1/4 cup (50g) granulated sugar
- 3 1/4 cups (400g) all-purpose flour, plus more for rolling
- 1 teaspoon salt
- 1 cup (225g) unsalted butter, cold

For the Chocolate Filling:

- 6 ounces (170g) dark chocolate, chopped or chocolate batons
- 1 egg, beaten (for egg wash)

Instructions:

1. Activate Yeast:

- In a bowl, combine lukewarm milk, active dry yeast, and sugar. Let it sit for 5-10 minutes until it becomes frothy.

2. Prepare Dough:

- In a large mixing bowl, combine the flour and salt. Make a well in the center and pour in the activated yeast mixture. Mix until it forms a dough.

3. Knead Dough:

- Turn the dough onto a floured surface and knead for about 5 minutes until it becomes smooth. Wrap the dough in plastic wrap and refrigerate for 1 hour.

4. Prepare Butter Layer:

- Roll out the chilled butter between two sheets of parchment paper to form a rectangle, roughly 10x7 inches (25x18 cm). Chill the butter layer in the refrigerator.

5. Laminate Dough:

    - Roll out the chilled dough on a floured surface into a rectangle, roughly 15x10 inches (38x25 cm). Place the chilled butter layer on two-thirds of the dough, then fold the uncovered third over the butter layer. Fold the other third over the top, creating three layers. This completes one fold. Chill the dough for 30 minutes.

6. Repeat Folds:

    - Repeat the rolling and folding process two more times, chilling the dough between each fold. This makes a total of three folds.

7. Final Rest:

    - After the final fold, wrap the dough in plastic wrap and refrigerate for at least 1 hour or overnight.

8. Roll and Shape:

    - Roll out the chilled dough on a floured surface into a large rectangle, about 1/4 inch (6 mm) thick. Cut the rectangle into smaller rectangles based on the size you desire for your pain au chocolat.

9. Add Chocolate:

    - Place chopped chocolate or chocolate batons on one end of each dough rectangle. Roll the dough over the chocolate to form a log.

10. Proofing:

    - Place the shaped pain au chocolat on a baking sheet, leaving space between each. Cover with a kitchen towel and let them proof at room temperature for 1-2 hours or until they double in size.

11. Preheat Oven:

    - Preheat your oven to 400°F (200°C).

12. Egg Wash:

- Brush the proofed pain au chocolat with the beaten egg wash.

13. Bake:

    - Bake in the preheated oven for 15-20 minutes or until the pain au chocolat is golden brown and puffed up.

14. Cool:

    - Allow the baked pain au chocolat to cool on a wire rack before serving.

15. Enjoy:

    - Serve these homemade pain au chocolat warm, with a cup of coffee or tea, and savor the delightful combination of flaky pastry and gooey chocolate!

Palmiers (Elephant Ears) Recipe

Ingredients:

- 1 cup granulated sugar
- 1/4 teaspoon salt
- 1 package puff pastry sheets (thawed if frozen)
- Extra sugar for sprinkling (optional)

Instructions:

1. Preheat Oven:

    - Preheat your oven to 400°F (200°C). Line a baking sheet with parchment paper.

2. Make Caramelized Sugar:

    - In a small bowl, mix together the granulated sugar and salt.

3. Roll Out Puff Pastry:

    - On a lightly floured surface, roll out the puff pastry into a rectangle.

4. Sprinkle Sugar:

    - Sprinkle half of the sugar mixture evenly over the puff pastry.

5. Fold and Sprinkle Again:

    - Starting from one side, fold the pastry towards the center. Repeat from the other side, so the folds meet in the middle. Sprinkle the remaining sugar mixture over the top.

6. Final Folding:

    - Fold the pastry in half again, creating a double fold. Press the folded layers together gently.

7. Chill:

    - Place the folded pastry in the refrigerator for about 15-20 minutes to firm up.

8. Slice:

- Take the chilled pastry out and slice it into 1/2-inch thick slices.

9. Arrange on Baking Sheet:

- Place the sliced palmiers on the prepared baking sheet, leaving space between each.

10. Bake:

- Bake in the preheated oven for 12-15 minutes or until the palmiers are golden brown and caramelized.

11. Cool:

- Allow the palmiers to cool on the baking sheet for a few minutes, then transfer them to a wire rack to cool completely.

12. Optional: Sugar Coating (Optional):

- If desired, you can sprinkle the baked palmiers with additional sugar while they are still warm.

13. Enjoy:

- Serve these delightful homemade palmiers with a cup of tea or coffee. Enjoy the crispy, caramelized layers of these sweet treats!

Palmiers, also known as Elephant Ears or French Hearts, are simple yet elegant pastries that are perfect for a sweet treat. The flaky, caramelized layers make them a delightful addition to any dessert table or afternoon tea.

Brioche Recipe

Ingredients:

For the Sponge:

- 1/4 cup (60 ml) warm whole milk
- 2 1/4 teaspoons (1 packet) active dry yeast
- 1/3 cup (40g) all-purpose flour

For the Dough:

- 3 1/4 cups (400g) all-purpose flour
- 1/4 cup (50g) granulated sugar
- 1 1/2 teaspoons salt
- 4 large eggs, room temperature
- 1 cup (225g) unsalted butter, softened

For Egg Wash:

- 1 egg, beaten with a pinch of salt

Instructions:

1. Activate Yeast:

   - In a small bowl, combine warm milk and active dry yeast. Let it sit for 5-10 minutes until it becomes frothy.

2. Make Sponge:

   - In a large bowl, mix the frothy yeast mixture with 1/3 cup of flour to create a sponge. Cover the bowl and let it rest for about 30 minutes.

3. Prepare Dough:

   - In the same bowl, add the remaining flour, sugar, and salt to the sponge. Mix well.

4. Add Eggs:

- Add the eggs, one at a time, mixing well after each addition.

5. Add Butter:

    - Gradually add the softened butter, mixing continuously until the dough is smooth and elastic. This can take about 10-15 minutes.

6. First Rise:

    - Cover the bowl with plastic wrap and let the dough rise in a warm place for 1-2 hours or until it doubles in size.

7. Shape and Second Rise:

    - Punch down the risen dough and shape it into a ball. Place the dough in a buttered and floured brioche pan or a regular loaf pan. Cover and let it rise for another 1-2 hours.

8. Preheat Oven:

    - Preheat your oven to 375°F (190°C).

9. Egg Wash:

    - Brush the risen dough with the beaten egg wash.

10. Bake:

    - Bake in the preheated oven for 25-30 minutes or until the brioche is golden brown and sounds hollow when tapped.

11. Cool:

    - Allow the brioche to cool in the pan for a few minutes, then transfer it to a wire rack to cool completely.

12. Enjoy:

    - Slice and enjoy your homemade brioche! Serve it plain, toasted, or with your favorite spreads.

Brioche is a rich and buttery bread that is perfect for breakfast or brunch. Its soft, slightly sweet, and tender crumb makes it a versatile and delightful treat. Whether enjoyed on its own or as the base for French toast or sandwiches, homemade brioche is a special and delicious addition to any table.

Galette des Rois (King Cake) Recipe

Ingredients:

For the Puff Pastry:

- 2 sheets of store-bought puff pastry (thawed, if frozen)

For the Almond Filling:

- 1 cup (100g) almond flour
- 1/2 cup (100g) granulated sugar
- 1/2 cup (115g) unsalted butter, softened
- 2 large eggs
- 1 teaspoon almond extract
- 1 tablespoon all-purpose flour

For Egg Wash:

- 1 egg, beaten with a pinch of salt

For Decoration:

- Powdered sugar (for dusting)

Instructions:

1. Preheat Oven:

- Preheat your oven to 400°F (200°C). Line a baking sheet with parchment paper.

2. Make Almond Filling:

- In a bowl, mix together almond flour, granulated sugar, softened butter, eggs, almond extract, and all-purpose flour until well combined. Set aside.

3. Roll Out Puff Pastry:

- Roll out one sheet of puff pastry into a round shape on a floured surface.

4. Add Almond Filling:

- Spread the almond filling evenly over the rolled-out puff pastry, leaving a border around the edges.

5. Insert the Bean or Figurine:

    - Place a small trinket, such as a dried bean or figurine, somewhere in the almond filling. Be sure to alert those enjoying the galette about its presence.

6. Seal with Second Puff Pastry:

    - Place the second sheet of puff pastry over the almond filling. Press the edges to seal and create a border.

7. Decorate:

    - Use a knife to create a decorative pattern on top of the galette. Be careful not to cut through the pastry completely.

8. Egg Wash:

    - Brush the top of the galette with the beaten egg wash.

9. Bake:

    - Bake in the preheated oven for 20-25 minutes or until the galette is golden brown and puffed up.

10. Cool:

    - Allow the galette to cool on a wire rack.

11. Dust with Powdered Sugar:

    - Once cooled, dust the galette with powdered sugar for an added touch.

12. Serve:

    - Cut into slices and serve. Tradition dictates that the person who finds the hidden trinket in their slice becomes the "king" or "queen" and is often crowned with a paper crown.

13. Enjoy:

   - Enjoy this delicious and festive Galette des Rois with family and friends, celebrating the Epiphany in true French style!

Galette des Rois is a traditional French pastry enjoyed during the Epiphany season. Filled with almond cream and often containing a hidden trinket, it's a delightful treat for sharing and celebrating with loved ones.

Cheese and Wine:

Cheese Fondue Recipe

Ingredients:

- 1 clove garlic, halved
- 1 cup dry white wine
- 1 tablespoon lemon juice
- 8 ounces (about 2 1/2 cups) Gruyère cheese, shredded
- 8 ounces (about 2 1/2 cups) Emmental cheese, shredded
- 1 tablespoon cornstarch
- 1/2 teaspoon dry mustard
- A pinch of nutmeg
- A pinch of black pepper
- 1 French baguette, cut into bite-sized cubes

Instructions:

1. Prepare Ingredients:

   - Shred the Gruyère and Emmental cheeses. Cut the garlic clove in half. Cut the French baguette into bite-sized cubes.

2. Rub the Pot with Garlic:

   - Rub the inside of a fondue pot with the halved garlic clove.

3. Make Wine Mixture:

   - In the fondue pot, heat the dry white wine and lemon juice over medium heat until it simmers. Be careful not to boil.

4. Toss Cheese with Cornstarch:

   - In a bowl, toss the shredded Gruyère and Emmental cheeses with cornstarch until evenly coated.

5. Add Cheese to Pot:

- Gradually add the cheese mixture to the simmering wine, stirring continuously in a figure-eight motion until the cheese is melted and smooth.

6. Season:

- Stir in the dry mustard, nutmeg, and black pepper. Continue stirring until the fondue is well combined and has a silky consistency.

7. Serve:

- Place the fondue pot on the fondue burner at the table. Adjust the heat to keep the fondue warm but not boiling.

8. Dip and Enjoy:

- Spear a piece of French baguette with a fondue fork, dip it into the melted cheese, and enjoy the classic cheese fondue experience.

9. Additional Dipping Ideas:

- Apart from bread, you can also offer a variety of dippables like apple slices, blanched vegetables, and even cured meats to dip into the delicious cheese fondue.

10. Keep Stirring:

- Stir the cheese fondue occasionally while serving to prevent it from separating.

11. Enjoy the Ritual:

- The fondue experience is not just about the delicious flavors but also about the communal act of dipping and sharing. Enjoy the social aspect of a cheese fondue gathering!

Cheese fondue is a classic Swiss dish that brings people together for a delightful and interactive dining experience. Enjoy the rich and creamy melted cheese with your favorite dippables, and savor the warmth and camaraderie of a fondue evening.

Raclette Recipe

Ingredients:

- Raclette cheese (1/2 to 1 pound per person)
- Boiled or steamed potatoes, sliced
- Pickles, gherkins, or pickled onions
- Cured meats such as ham, prosciutto, or salami
- Fresh vegetables, like cherry tomatoes or bell pepper strips
- Crusty bread, sliced
- Olive oil (for dipping bread)
- Optional: Mustard or other condiments

Equipment:

- Raclette grill or raclette machine

Instructions:

1. Prepare Ingredients:

- Slice the raclette cheese into thin, even slices. Arrange the boiled or steamed potato slices, pickles, cured meats, fresh vegetables, and sliced bread on a serving platter.

2. Heat the Raclette Grill:

- Preheat the raclette grill or raclette machine according to the manufacturer's instructions.

3. Melt the Cheese:

- Place slices of raclette cheese onto the raclette grill trays. Slide the trays under the grill, and let the cheese melt until it's bubbly and slightly browned.

4. Serve with Accompaniments:

- While the cheese is melting, encourage your guests to start assembling their plates with a variety of accompaniments.

5. Scrape and Enjoy:

- Once the cheese is melted, use a spatula or scraper to scrape the gooey cheese onto the plate over the chosen accompaniments.

6. Continue Melting Cheese:

- Repeat the process, melting more cheese as needed, until everyone is satisfied.

7. Add Olive Oil Dip for Bread:

- If you have sliced bread, offer a small bowl of olive oil for dipping.

8. Optional Condiments:

- Provide mustard or other condiments for extra flavor if desired.

9. Enjoy the Raclette Experience:

- Enjoy the interactive and social aspect of raclette dining. The melted cheese pairs wonderfully with the variety of accompaniments.

10. Note:

- Raclette can be a leisurely and convivial meal, so take your time and savor each cheesy bite.

11. Dessert Raclette (Optional):

- For a sweet twist, consider melting chocolate on the raclette grill and serve it with fruit, marshmallows, or cubes of cake for dessert.

Raclette is a delightful and sociable meal where friends and family gather around a table, melting cheese and enjoying a variety of accompaniments. The interactive nature of raclette makes it a fun and memorable dining experience.

Fromage Blanc Recipe

Ingredients:

- 1 quart (4 cups) whole milk
- 2 tablespoons cultured buttermilk or fromage blanc (as a starter culture)
- Cheesecloth
- Salt (optional, to taste)

Instructions:

1. Heat the Milk:

- Pour the whole milk into a large, heavy-bottomed pot. Heat the milk over medium heat, stirring frequently, until it reaches a temperature of around 180°F (82°C). This helps to denature the proteins in the milk.

2. Cool the Milk:

- Allow the milk to cool down to around 110°F (43°C). You can speed up the cooling process by placing the pot in a cold water bath.

3. Add the Starter Culture:

- Add 2 tablespoons of cultured buttermilk or fromage blanc to the cooled milk. Stir well to distribute the starter culture evenly.

4. Incubate:

- Cover the pot with a lid and let it sit undisturbed at room temperature for about 12-24 hours. During this time, the milk will thicken and set into a soft curd.

5. Check for Curd Formation:

- After the incubation period, check for the formation of a soft curd. It should have a yogurt-like consistency.

6. Cut and Drain the Curd:

- Cut the curd into small cubes using a knife. Allow the curds to drain by gently transferring them to a cheesecloth-lined colander or a fine-mesh strainer. Let the whey drain off for 6-12 hours, or until the desired thickness is achieved.

7. Salt (Optional):

- If desired, you can mix salt into the drained curds to taste. This step is optional and depends on your preference.

8. Transfer to Storage Container:

- Transfer the fromage blanc to a clean container for storage.

9. Refrigerate:

- Refrigerate the fromage blanc for a few hours before serving. This allows it to firm up and develop its flavor.

10. Enjoy:

- Fromage blanc is now ready to be enjoyed! Serve it on its own, with fresh fruit, or as a topping for crackers.

Note:

- Fromage blanc can be used in both sweet and savory dishes. Experiment with adding herbs, honey, or fruit for different flavor profiles.

Storage:

- Store the fromage blanc in the refrigerator. Consume it within a week for the best flavor and texture.

Tip:

- Save a couple of tablespoons from your first batch to use as a starter culture for future batches. This helps maintain the consistency of your homemade fromage blanc.

Quiche Alsacienne (Alsatian Bacon and Onion Tart) Recipe

Ingredients:

For the Tart Dough:

- 1 1/4 cups all-purpose flour
- 1/2 cup unsalted butter, cold and cut into small cubes
- 1/4 teaspoon salt
- 1/4 cup ice water

For the Filling:

- 6 slices bacon, diced
- 1 large onion, thinly sliced
- 1 tablespoon unsalted butter
- 1 cup heavy cream
- 3 large eggs
- Salt and pepper, to taste
- A pinch of nutmeg
- 1 cup Gruyère cheese, grated

Instructions:

1. Prepare Tart Dough:

- In a food processor, combine the flour, cold butter cubes, and salt. Pulse until the mixture resembles coarse crumbs. Add ice water gradually while pulsing until the dough comes together.

2. Form Tart Dough:

- Turn the dough out onto a floured surface and form it into a disc. Wrap it in plastic wrap and refrigerate for at least 30 minutes.

3. Preheat Oven:

- Preheat your oven to 375°F (190°C).

4. Roll Out Dough:

- Roll out the chilled dough on a floured surface to fit a tart pan. Press the dough into the pan and trim the edges. Prick the bottom with a fork.

5. Blind Bake:

- Line the tart shell with parchment paper and fill it with pie weights or dried beans. Blind bake for 15 minutes. Remove the weights and parchment, and bake for an additional 5 minutes or until lightly golden.

6. Prepare Filling:

- In a skillet, cook the diced bacon until crisp. Remove the bacon and sauté the sliced onions in the bacon fat with butter until soft and golden.

7. Whisk Egg Mixture:

- In a bowl, whisk together the heavy cream, eggs, salt, pepper, and nutmeg.

8. Assemble Quiche:

- Spread the cooked bacon and onions over the pre-baked tart shell. Pour the egg mixture over the bacon and onions.

9. Add Gruyère Cheese:

- Sprinkle the grated Gruyère cheese evenly over the top.

10. Bake:

- Bake in the preheated oven for 25-30 minutes or until the quiche is set and the top is golden brown.

11. Cool and Serve:

- Allow the quiche to cool slightly before slicing. Serve warm and enjoy the delicious flavors of Quiche Alsacienne!

Note:

- Quiche Alsacienne is traditionally served with a green salad on the side.

Optional:

- Customize the quiche by adding caramelized onions, mushrooms, or herbs according to your taste preferences.

Cheese Board with Baguette

Cheese Selection:

Brie:
- Creamy and mild, Brie offers a soft and velvety texture.

Camembert:
- Similar to Brie but with a stronger flavor and a creamy interior.

Gouda:
- A semi-hard cheese with a nutty flavor and smooth texture.

Blue Cheese:
- Choose a blue cheese like Roquefort or Gorgonzola for a bold and tangy addition.

Cheddar:
- Opt for a sharp or aged cheddar for a robust flavor.

Goat Cheese (Chevre):
- Creamy and tangy, goat cheese adds variety to the board.

Manchego:
- A firm Spanish cheese made from sheep's milk, offering a nutty and slightly sweet taste.

Gruyère:
- A Swiss cheese with a smooth texture and a sweet, slightly salty flavor.

Accompaniments:

Baguette:
- Slice a fresh baguette into thin pieces for pairing with the cheeses.

Crackers:
- Include a variety of crackers such as water crackers, whole grain, and flavored options.

Fresh Fruits:
- Grapes, apple slices, and figs complement the cheese with sweetness and texture.

Nuts:
- Almonds, walnuts, or pecans add a crunchy element to the board.

Dried Fruits:
- Apricots, dates, or raisins provide a chewy and sweet contrast.

Honey or Fruit Preserves:

- Drizzle honey over the cheeses or include fruit preserves for a touch of sweetness.

Olives:
- A selection of olives, such as green and black varieties, adds a savory note.

Cured Meats:
- Salami, prosciutto, or chorizo complement the cheeses with their savory flavors.

Mustards:
- Whole-grain mustard or Dijon mustard adds a zesty kick.

Presentation Tips:

Arrange in Groups:
- Group similar cheeses together for an organized presentation.

Texture Variation:
- Place soft cheeses, hard cheeses, and blue cheeses in separate sections for visual appeal.

Colorful Display:
- Incorporate colorful fruits, olives, and dried fruits for a visually appealing spread.

Cheese Knives:
- Provide appropriate cheese knives for each type of cheese.

Labeling:
- Consider labeling each cheese to help guests identify their favorites.

Aesthetic Balance:
- Aim for a balance of flavors, textures, and colors across the entire board.

Room Temperature:
- Allow the cheeses to come to room temperature before serving for the best flavors.

Wine Pairing:
- Serve with a selection of red and white wines that complement the cheese varieties.

Creating a cheese board with a variety of textures, flavors, and accompaniments ensures a delightful and visually appealing experience for your guests. Customize the selection based on your preferences and enjoy the art of pairing different elements on your cheese board.

www.ingramcontent.com/pod-product-compliance
Lightning Source LLC
LaVergne TN
LVHW081552060526
838201LV00054B/1870